D1556418

Foundations of Writing Kit

Part 1 Learning to Write

Designed to support the implementation of this Report, the Kit offers a practical approach to the development of the child as a competent writer. The methods, developed by teachers in Scotland, blend the results of the most recent studies of the way children learn to write with the best classroom practice. In addition to a further copy of the Report and a comprehensive Teacher's Handbook, the Kit contains a range of classroom materials, games, activities and programmes which support: the development of the language of writing; the teaching of handwriting; the beginning of writing; the group organisation of writing; finding things to write about; putting writing to use; writing in the wider curriculum; teacher response to writing.

AN ORDER FORM FOR THE KIT APPEARS AT THE END OF THIS BOOK

CONSULTATIVE COMMITTEE ON THE CURRICULUM

FOUNDATIONS OF WRITING

THE REPORT OF A PROJECT
ON THE TEACHING OF WRITING
AT THE EARLY STAGES.

COMMITTEE ON PRIMARY EDUCATION

First published 1986
Scottish Curriculum Development Service, Edinburgh Centre
ISBN 0 947942 90 4

REPRODUCTION
It is hoped that this document will provide information
which can be used by those responsible for organising
Pre-service and In-service Training. To this end, the
Committee on Primary Education hereby give permission
for the document to be reproduced either in whole or
in part, provided that due acknowledgement is made of
the source.

Additional copies of the document are available from:
Principal Curriculum Development Officer (Primary Education)
Scottish Curriculum Development Service
Moray House College of Education
Holyrood Road
Edinburgh EH8 8AQ

Typeset by Whitelaw & Palmer Ltd, Glasgow

Printed and bound in Scotland by Russell Print, Blantyre.

CONTENTS

FOREWORD

This paper was presented to the Committee on Primary Education (COPE) as the final Report of the Steering Comittee and Project Team of the Foundations of Writing Project, the aims of which are stated in Section 1. As the work undertaken was a direct result of ideas put forward in "Hand in your Writing" (1981), the report has been authorised for publication as a CCC Implementation Paper.

Acting for the CCC, COPE warmly welcomed the direction and impetus the Report gives to the teaching of writing at the early stages of Primary Education. It is the view of COPE that the Report describes a more effective approach to the teaching of writing which has implications for teachers and pupils at all stages of the primary school. The findings of the Project and recommendations that the Report makes will be of interest and relevance to practising teachers and to their colleagues in promoted posts, in the advisory services and in Colleges of Education.

The ideas and suggestions proposed for the implementation of the underlying philosophy can be put into practice using materials that are readily available in schools, but there will also be packs of teaching materials which can be obtained by schools from the Learning Resources Unit at Jordanhill College of Education. The first of these packs is currently available at a cost of £57 to schools in Scotland. During a three year period a limited evaluation will be conducted.

A major strength of the Project is that it has always been firmly located in the reality of the work in schools. The CCC is greatly indebted to the Project Directors and the Steering Committee for their inspiration and leadership, to the advisers, promoted staff and teachers involved for their co-operation and constructive criticism, and to the children whose work gives the reality and purpose to the overall Project and to the pages that follow.

Dan Taylor
Interim Chairman, COPE

August 1986

1. BACKGROUND TO THE PROJECT

The Project originated in the Scottish Committee on Language Arts (SCOLA) publication "Hand in your Writing" which, in its discussion of the teaching of writing, expressed misgivings about the writing ability of children in Scottish primary schools. This drew on the examination of a large sample of writing produced by children in the P4 to P7 range. The publication accepted that the majority of Scottish children learn to write if this means the ability to form letters, put these letters into words and these words into sentences with a reasonable degree of correctness. However, children's writing ability seemed inadequate to express their own experiences and imaginings or to support the demands of school. SCOLA believed that the roots of this limited competence lay in the way writing was taught throughout the school and did not simply emerge in the later stages. It was decided to look at how writing might be taught in the first three years of primary education.

The Committee on Primary Education (COPE) accepted a proposal for such a Project. Its remit was to develop materials and techniques to support the teaching of writing in P1 to P3. It was not seen as a research project. The large number of variables present meant that an objective assessment was not possible. Evaluation would depend on the judgement of experienced teachers. A small number of "evaluation" schools were included in the later stages of the Project. Their role was not to evaluate the materials as such but to assess if they could be used by class teachers who had access to no other information about the Project.

An approach was made to three regional authorities for permission to work in their areas. Meetings were then held with primary advisers who suggested possible schools. Subsequent meetings were held with promoted staff in these schools and with classroom teachers. Although the schools participating were not self-selective but were invited to take part in the Project it was made clear at all stages that the Project was not being imposed on any school. The school had to be willing to accept it.

Primary Advisers were assigned to supervise the work of the Project in the sixteen selected schools and to set up machinery for liaison between the schools. Unfortunately industrial action reduced the possibilities for bringing school staffs together.

Jordanhill seconded two lecturers to work part-time with the Project, one as co-director and the other as an area supervisor. A national steering committee was set up representing the schools and the other agencies involved in the Project. The Development Group on Language Arts established by COPE to conclude various Projects initiated by SCOLA maintained a watching brief. The work of the Project was supported by the Scottish Curriculum Development Service at Moray House College of Education.

Meetings were held with parents to explain what was intended, to indicate the nature of the work that children might bring home and to provide background to the reports that children might give of what they had been doing in schools. Many of these meetings were lively and helpful and in some cases opened up useful areas of co-operation between home and school.

Making a start

Meetings of teachers were held before the Project started in the schools. At these meetings the present state of writing in the schools was discussed and certain propositions were presented to the teachers for their consideration. The initial work of the Project was based on what was discussed at these meetings. Although these basic awarenesses were to be much modified and extended by teachers during their three years' work with the Project, they did illuminate the work of the Project and will be represented in this report.

Although the Project produced a body of classroom-tested material the Project is not about material. It is about certain awarenesses about the written language and how children acquire it. The material may help a teacher make a transition from one way of teaching writing to another but once the basic principles of the Project are accepted teachers will find it comparatively simple to develop their own material or to incorporate these principles in their ongoing work.

The role of teachers in the Project was not simply to test material devised outside the school. Teachers and Project staff were partners who together worked out new approaches to the teaching of writing and materials and situations to sustain these approaches. No matter how theoretically attractive certain approaches might be they were discarded if they proved difficult to work in the classroom. Throughout the Project the directors, as much as the teachers, were required to question the assumptions with which they entered into this work.

To look at the material used in 1981 and at the current version is to see a refining and streamlining; to read the various papers distributed by the Project team over these years is to see a corresponding refinement in the ideas that animate the Project work.

The success of work in schools during the Project depended on teachers engaging in this questioning of assumptions and the resulting practice and in their actively modifying and expanding the Project material to meet new objectives and their own situations. Development in curricular practice is most effective when the necessity for change is accepted from within and not imposed from without.

This report hopes that other teachers will also question their assumptions about the teaching of writing. The material will support such teachers as they move towards what teachers working within the Project agree is an effective way of teaching young children to write.

The report poses certain questions about the teaching of writing and attempts to enunciate certain principles about that teaching which teachers agreed are important. Once the staff of a school have read and considered the report these questions may provide a check-list against which a school may evaluate its teaching of writing.

The following report records a co-operative effort involving teachers, advisers, lecturers and representatives of the local authorities.

All contributed – all learned.

2. "COPY IT INTO YOUR WRITING JOTTERS"

The Project directors worked in co-operation with many teachers during the Project. They visited many classrooms, watched teachers and children at work and worked with children. There were many long and frank discussions.

The classrooms visited were bright, lively and active places. Children were obviously happy at school and the relationship between them and their teachers was good. The teachers obviously accepted a view of education that was active, child-centred and experiential. It was strange that the teaching of writing seemed to run counter to much else that they did.

The picture of the teaching of writing at P1 which follows lays no claim to present the only approach which may be met in schools. It represents a "worst-case" picture and many teachers may feel their own practice is more advanced than this. It is hoped that all teachers will recognise in it at least some of the realities of their own classroom – and hovering always in the background must be the question: "Just how effective is this teaching?"

We open the door and sit down.

There the class sat looking at the teacher as she worked at the blackboard. Perhaps she was writing up that day's news.

"Today is a wet day."

Slowly and carefully the teacher built up this "story" letter by letter giving a com mentary as she went.

". . . now be careful to take the long stroke of the 'd' right down until it touches the line . . . now take your writing jotters and copy down today's story . . . remember, we want neat writing today . . . and when you're finished you can draw me a nice picture of you playing in the rain . . . what might you be doing? . . . that's right, you might be splashing in the puddles.

Now, I am coming first to hear the Pied Pipers read so will they get their reading books out. No noise, please."

The non-Pied Pipers started to copy out the day's story, slowly and carefully, possibly with tongues purposefully extended. There would be many starts and stops and much looking up at the board and down at the page. Children probably found their own ways of producing letters neatly once the teacher was engaged else where – draw a stroke up from the line and add a circle to produce that neat 'd'.

And so the day's story was produced. It would be inspected by the teacher, and, if the child had copied it neatly, it would be taken home to be shown to parents who approved of this activity. After all, its efficiency could not be called in question because demonstrably the child could write and besides, that's how the parents had been taught to write.

Our imaginary P1 teacher would have ways of supplementing her newscopy with other "writing" activities designed to give the children table-work and, at the same time, improve their ability to form letters. Children might be given writing-patterns to copy or letters to trace. Work books in which some letters were already partly formed might also be used and given the status of "work" as opposed to "play". And so, in a variety of ways "writing", or rather the practising of letter-formation, could take up a remarkably high proportion of the child's unsuper-vised work time.

Since these activities kept children busy and quiet, teachers might claim that they helped give them the work-habit.

Since this approach appeared to have worked over the years and to be acceptable to parents and teachers alike, teachers might legitimately ask why they *should* change their practice.

3. THE NEED FOR CHANGE

Our teacher at the board concentrated on handwriting skills – letter formation, neatness, directionality, spaces between words and so on. She taught as she did because she based her approach to writing on a philosophy which differed significantly from that which the Project finally developed.

The fact that she chose not to concern herself with such matters as the purpose in writing, how the written sentence is built up and the "meaningfulness" of what is being written does not mean that these are not involved in even the simplest piece of writing. In the absence of any reference to them by the teacher children will have to grapple with the understanding of them for themselves.

We have to remember that the children do not just learn what the teacher chooses to teach; they will try to make sense out of all the items present in a learning situation. Children cannot be put in a non-learning situation. They will learn but perhaps not what the teacher might wish.

"Today is a wet day" is a simple statement yet even in the teaching of such a state ment there is an ignoring of several things.

Why has this to be written?

For whom is it written?

Why has it to be written in this way?

How "meaningful" is the statement?

If the statement "Today is a wet day" were to be read tomorrow, next week or a hundred years from today, would it make any sense?

As the child's writing increases in complexity then the child's understanding of the purposes, functions and processes of writing becomes vitally important.

It is easy to be concerned with the appearance of writing – how it looks on the page – and to ignore the substance of writing, what processes are involved when a child writes and the quality of the meanings the writing expresses.

Writing is like an iceberg – only a small part of the whole writing process appears above the surface. Beneath the marks on the paper lie many awarenesses and many decisions.

These are the composing skills.

They are more important than handwriting skills.

They are often seen a being "a gift".

They may be untaught in schools.

Our teacher has to

(a) identify what children have to know if they are to become effective writers;

(b) help children to acquire helpful criteria or else they will believe that writing is only about neatness, carefulness and correctness;

(c) start to teach writing through what is important to the child – the need to express something meaningful – not through letter formation which is a technical, non-intellectual skill;

(d) help children appreciate that, unlike speech, a written statement has to contain within itself sufficient information to make it understandable without reference to something else;

(e) accept that she is not even teaching handwriting, the main object of her teaching, in an effective way but in a way that will encourage the development of bad habits which will be difficult to get rid of later.

The teacher had a limited view of what she had to teach in order to help her children to be writers. This view of writing derived from the advice she had received throughout her teaching career. To her, at most, writing expressed the child's personal life or was a vehicle for carrying round information to service various subject areas. She had never been asked to consider the potential of writing for the exploration and organisation of experience. She had not been asked to consider the opportunity that writing gives for reflection on experience or the relationship between the written language and the child's intellectual functioning. She did not see the written language as a source of power.

This is a view of writing which has been little considered until recently, but it is one which the Project believes to be fundamental to the teaching of writing in the early stages.

The teacher had been led to believe that the teaching of writing was essentially the teaching of the mechanics of writing, handwriting skills; all else would develop spontaneously or be taught later.

Alerting children to all that the written language can do cannot be postponed until later. The uninvolved and superficial writing at the upper primary level examined in "Hand in Your Writing" is a product of a failure to lay the foundations of writing in the early stages.

The Foundations of Writing Project

The Foundations of Writing Project reacted to the need for change by developing, with teachers, a strategy for the teaching of writing, which, because of the fundamental questions teachers asked, became as much about *how we teach as how we teach writing* and for many experienced teachers the "excitement" of the Project for them derived from the significant changes which they made in their classroom practice throughout most curricular areas.

The Project made available to teachers current knowledge about the purposes and functions of writing. It sought to define what children need to learn in order to be effective writers. It emphasised the knowledge about language, especially the written language, that children bring to the learning process and describes the mechanisms through which children learn language.

The Project accepted the crucial role of the teacher in any learning situation. The Project sought to define the teacher's role more precisely and help the teacher to motivate children to write by providing starting points, neutral situations and contexts which children may inhabit with their own experiences. The experience of the child is valued. The Project seeks to show how certain writing tasks, e.g. the ubiquitous newstime, can create difficulties for young children and discusses in some detail the kind of consistent response which helps children to develop their own writing criteria. It gives phases of development, significant areas, markers which help the teacher assess where the child is in writing and suggests possible future work. It allows for work that is really child-centred, individualised and differentiated.

The Project produced material which was not concerned simply with the develop ment of writing skills. It recognised the centrality of language and the close relationship between the written language and the child's intellectual functioning and sought to incorporate writing within the other activities of the classroom. The Project valued expressive and experiential activities, recognising not only their own intrinsic values, but also the fact that they encouraged various skills and awarenesses that were relevant to writing competence. The Project drew on familiar materials and reorganised them so that they involved the children more deeply, made greater demands on them, made them concentrate longer and helped them regard these activities as serious "work". The Project's clear definition of teaching objectives within these activities led teachers to regard them more seriously and helped them develop a more coherent programme of work. The Project demonstrated how activities like drawing, plasticine work, modelling, sandplay, etc. could become techniques through which children investigated, recorded and communicated their recall of experience or the products of their imagining.

This helped ease the pressure of time in that children were prepared to work more purposefully on these activities for longer periods of time. The teacher could use existing classroom activities to develop writing skills and did not have to add new activities to an over-loaded programme.

The Project questioned the assumption of most early stages practice that it is essential for the teacher to find time to teach directly to children on a one to one basis in the area of "basic skills". Of course, there are occasions on which such a relationship is vital but it is only possible to sustain this in a limited way. Teachers only have to consider the time at their disposal and the number of children in the class to appreciate that only limited one-to-one working is possible. The Project however sought to explore the potential of the *group* as the writing unit. Not as a series of individuals waiting to enter into individual discussion with the teacher but as a more efficient means by which the teacher shares her criteria and expectations with the whole group.

Let us now look at some of the questions that arose during the Project about the teaching of writing.

4. QUESTIONS TO BE ASKED ABOUT THE TEACHING OF WRITING

Most of the questions began by looking at the kind of teaching going on in our imaginary classroom.

(i) Do children learn language like that?

The children in our imaginary class were being taught imitatively – they copied from the board.

They were being taught prescriptively – the teacher gave them various rules and precepts.

If children don't learn language skills like that how do they learn?

Children learn

actively, systematically, creatively.

actively
they use language in a series of contexts that give helpful feedback;

systematically
from the language data around them they internalise a series of rules which enables them to generate language;

creatively
they rediscover for themselves the rules governing language.

Of course children's rules are not always adult rules, e.g. "I goed my bike", but they allow children to use language within groups. These rules will be used until the language data encountered causes them to discard those rules and construct new ones.

Teachers may have to ask themselves how children's learning could be active, systematic and creative.

(ii) Do we build on what children know?
The teacher at the board may not consider that children bring very much knowledge that is of relevance to learning to write. We have seen her ignoring those mechanisms through which a child acquires language and teaching through imitation and prescription.

Children know that the printed word tells stories.

(a) The child knows what a story is for. Telling a story to someone may give writing a clearer purpose for children. It's easier to understand that stories can divert or entertain people who will read them or hear them than that stories will tell someone, somewhere, that "Today is a wet day".

Children know how stories work. People tell them stories or read stories to them. They listen to them on cassettes. Cartoons and comic strips tell stories.

Children have some idea of how a story builds up. They have some idea of human types, wicked wolf, kind princess, and of human motivation. Stories describe people and places. Stories use direct speech.

The child has picked up some formal items – "Once upon a time . . ." and "They lived happily ever after."

Children are in control in the story. They do not have to try and recall what actually happened – they can make things happen or not happen. Through stories children can inhabit other people, other places, other experiences.

Stories have meaning for children in a way that the recall of first-hand experience has not. In speech it is rare for a child to have to give a sustained recall of past events without the support and stimulus of questions and comments. It is more common for a child to have to carry a story, a joke or a riddle on its own in speech. There is a more natural carry-over from a child telling a story in speech to writing a story.

The Project uses the story-form even when the child is supposed to be recalling an experience. Strict veracity is not important.

It may even help the young children when they writes not to be compelled to recall what actually happened. Children can be *more* expressive for they can write about people who may be afraid or embarrassed as they are but without admitting that the story is about themselves.

Later the report will discuss how the story-form has to be modified when children are reporting on observations and investigations.

(b) Teachers spoke with regret of the limited experience that children might have of the written word in their own homes. Here they were thinking of what might be called "literary" forms and ignoring other forms of print.

Teachers were aware that children are more influenced today by sounds and visual images and that the world outside school may no longer support the acquisition of literacy as it once did.

Despite this, what knowledge of the printed word might a child have?

In the home the child is surrounded by print. All forms of packaging, television, brochures, catalogues, letters carry the printed word.

And that is just inside the house!

Think of the signs and posters which surround children outside, especially in an urban environment.

Children have considerable awareness of the printed word. Are we to suppose that children with their need to make sense of what goes on around them will wait until they come to school before beginning to think about what this writing is for?

The very least a child will understand is that the written word is not an object in itself. Writing is not like a pattern on a wallpaper. It contains meanings.

Children coming to school may understand something about writing, or the printed word. The most important thing is that it contains meanings and, if they are lucky, they will appreciate that these meanings have to do with experiences that will interest, amuse, thrill them.

(c) However, what many children will not have seen, is anyone actually producing all this print. There are all the words in all their various contexts but it may be only in letters or lists written at home that the child sees the processes involved in writing.

The child can relate to the end-product of writing but may have no idea how one sets about producing it. This is where the teacher will have to concentrate his/her teaching.

The child needs more than stimulus or praise. Through involvement with other writers – teacher, other children, authors and through the demonstration of writing by others – children learn what they have to do when they write.

(iii) Do we teach too many things at the one time?

The child can only pay attention to the demands of a limited number of tasks at one time.

Because there has been little consideration or analysis of what is involved in writing the child copying from the board has to pay attention to too many things at one time.

The child has to:

learn a number of letter shapes which have been chosen not because they have common characteristics but because they appear in that day's news story;

cope with directionality, spaces between words, relative starting points;

put words into sentence structures which conceivably could be ones not commonly used in speech, especially if they are derived from reading schemes;

cope with the relationship between sound and letter shape;

cope with such meaning as there is.

All of these things are quite casually included in one activity without serious consideration of their relative difficulty or if the mastering of one skill inhibits the mastering of another.

The Project would not attempt to teach handwriting skills at the same time as skills which have to do with thought processes. Composing and handwriting skills are taught separately.

If children are learning handwriting skills at the same time as learning how to compose a story it will be the composition which will suffer.

As we have said, our teacher at the board may believe she is teaching handwriting skills but all these other things are there and children have to make their own sense of them.

(iv) Do children learn good habits?

The teacher would hope that this careful copying would lead to good habits being formed. But even in that very area which the teacher sees as being important potential harm is being done. Children are encouraged to form letters carefully and slowly when they should be being trained to form letters quickly so that there is the minimal impeding of the thinking processes involved in writing. The continual reference to the board inteferes with their development of fluency in writing. Many children sitting round tables have to turn their heads to the board and they may naturally reverse the letters in consequence. Left on their own while the teacher works with another group, the Pied Pipers, they may develop "easy" ways of forming letters which will hinder the efficient formation and linking-up of letters.

This "slow and careful" way of teaching handwriting skills may be the cause of handwriting problems later on.

The Project spends a lot of time on the teaching of handwriting skills so that children learn as soon a possible to write quickly and legibly, then to concentrate their resources on the more difficult task of composing what they want to express and communicate.

(v) Are we teaching what children need?
Teachers teaching writing are interested in letter formation and other aspects of handwriting, in sound/letter correspondence, in phonetic values, in spelling and in "correct" grammar.

Most of their talk and much of their instruction will be about these things.

What interests a child in language is that it means things. The child is interested in meanings. These get things done.

What meaning has copying the news got for a child? "Today is a wet day." The "story" is meaningless. Of course it's not gibberish but why is it being written and who will read it?

Of course the activity has meaning for the teacher; who sees it all from an adult perspective. It's all part of learning to write. The purpose will be made clear at a later date but young children live in a "now" world.

Learning to write has to be made meaningful for the child.

(vi) Do we develop helpful criteria?
In an examination of the total writing output of a number of P1 classes the Project team discovered that teachers' comments could be a generalised encouragement or related to quality of letter formation or neatness.

Admonitions during the teaching of writing were frequently about "taking time: being careful; making a neat job."

The Project team discussed with a number of older children who had just written a story what it was they thought their teacher would value. They found it difficult to say.

"Correctness and neatness" were mentioned as were "good words" or "saying what it felt like". There was even the mention of the story having "to be long enough."

If children are going to write well they will have to have some understanding of what is expected of them when they write.

These criteria will be formed on the basis of children's awareness of the writing of others and the responses others make to their writing.

What criteria will the children form on the basis of the blackboard lesson?

Not that writing is meaningful.
Not that writing has to have a purpose.
Not that writing has to communicate.

They will think only that writing has to be done carefully, neatly and correctly if that is all the teacher has talked to them about.

After all, what meaning has "Today is a wet day" got out of the context of today?

These questions having been asked about current practice, it became clearer what children had to learn to become efficient writers.

5. FINDING WHAT HAS TO BE LEARNED

What did the Project actually do?

With the beginning writer –

A variety of expressive activities developed skills relevant to writing.

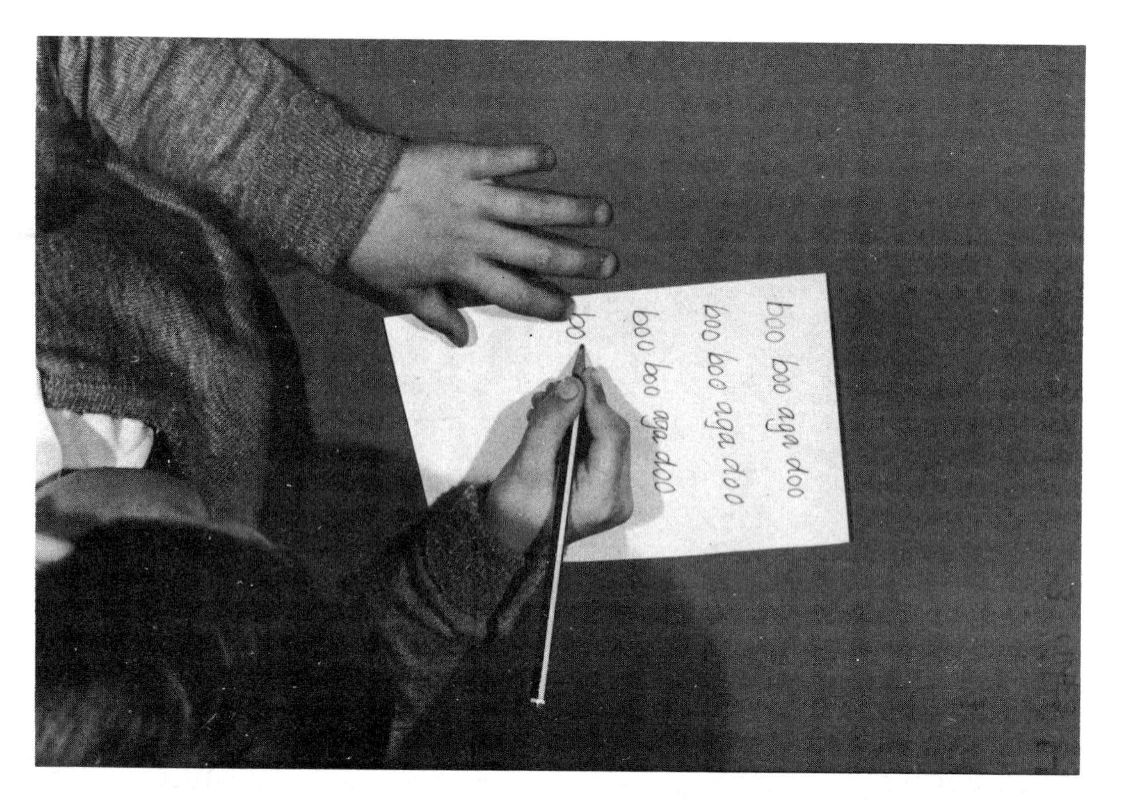

The child developed a legible and fluent writing skill but the teaching of handwriting was separate from development of the composing skills.

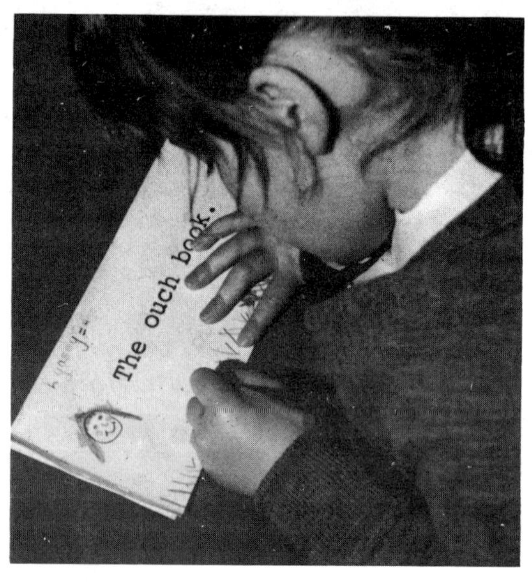

The child began to write using various means.

An examination of both traditional and creative approaches to the teaching of writing showed that little attention had been paid to the teaching of the processes involved in writing. It was clear, looking at writing throughout the primary school, as the SCOLA documents indicate, that children tackled writing tasks with skills and awarenesses more appropriate to speech. Where would these awarenesses and tasks be identified?

(a) Talking and writing

Teachers were asked to consider children talking and writing, to look at photographs of children talking in groups and of children writing.

What can be learned from the consideration of these photographs which might help teachers define what they have to do to help children become writers?

(i) The child talking is supported by the **context** within which talking takes place. This context is both physical and human. The purpose in talking is usually clear. The context may actually provide the content for the conversation/discussion/argument. The other participants support and encourage the child by comments and responses. The other participants in the conversation share in the maintaining of the conversation.

(ii) In talk the **audience** is there. The audience through its responses and questions lets the child know if what is being said is interesting, relevant, comprehensible.

(iii) The spoken language may be **less explicit** than the written language; facial expression, gesture, tone of voice, etc. may carry meaning; the child may actually point to items within the context to support what is being said.

(iv) There is a **shared experience** since the child's audience will probably know about the experience being communicated and if there is any doubt questions can be asked.

(v) The spoken language is **less explicit** and **less structured** than written language. Spoken communications are improvised as the conversation goes on.

(vi) There are **few opportunities for reflection**; as others share in the conversation the child may have little control over the direction the conversation takes; participants in speech situations seem tolerant of digressions and repetitions, perhaps the warmth of human conversation compensates for these; perhaps the limited opportunity for reflection offered by speech means that the speaker has to come to a more precise articulation of the meanings he/she wishes to express by having to go over them several times in the course of the conversation.

In contrast, the writing child may not enjoy the support provided by the context within which speech takes place.

Writing may be a solitary activity.

(i) The child will have to define to him/herself the purpose in writing.

(ii) From his/her own recollections or imaginings he/she will have to find the content to support that purpose.

(iii) In the absence of immediate feedback from his readers the child may have to decide for him/herself what readers need to know or would like to know.

(iv) The child has to find a way of expressing all this in a way which is appropriate to writing.

(v) The child has to communicate through a medium, handwriting, which to many children is awkward, if not difficult.

(vi) The child has to meet certain expectations about correctness in spelling, punctuation and grammar.

(vii) Because the reader cannot ask eliciting questions there will have to be a degree of explicitness in writing which is not necessary in talk.

(viii) Because reading is more difficult than listening the digressive nature of talk would not be tolerated in writing.

The writing child has to find within his/her own resources the support which the speech context would help supply. She/he also has to generate a form of language which is *more explicit and coherent* than the spoken language. The Project sought to give that support by teaching writing as a group and not as an individual activity. Within the Project writing was a public activity.

The speaking child may usually find or refine his/her meanings in conversation with others. The separation of writing from action allows opportunities for reflection.

(b) Component skills in writing

When the various skills and awarenesses that a child employs in writing are examined they can be seen to fall into two groups.

(i) One group has to do with the composing of what has to be expressed and communicated.

Here the child has to make decisions about the following:

Why am I writing?

What will I select from all I might say to serve the purposes of the writing?

What will the people who will read this need to be told or might want to be told?

What words and structures will I select that will satisfy me and convey what I have to say clearly and effectively?

Will the people for whom I am writing expect my piece of writing to be communicated in a particular form?

These are composing skills.
They are higher-order skills because they involve children with decisions they have to make for themselves.

(ii) The other group of skills has to do with getting all this on paper:

handwriting
spelling
punctuation
grammaticality

Children don't have to make decisions here – they have to follow the rules. They may get the rules wrong but they cannot decide to change them.

These are the "secretarial" skills.
They are lower-order skills because they depend on the child's conforming to rules.

School practice tends to concentrate its attention on the lower order skills.

The Project concentrates on composing skills but ensures the secretarial skills are adequate for the needs of a young writer.

When the various skills and awarenesses which contribute to writing were examined the question was asked: "Is writing a specific activity or does it share skills with other activities?"

Obviously certain skills, like handwriting, spelling and punctuation, are specific to the written language and writing shares vocabulary and structural elements with the spoken language but many of the awarenesses which go towards the composing skills are employed by the child in other forms of expression – skills of perception, quality of response to experience, the ability to impose order on experiences – these will exist outside writing.

It should be possible to develop in the child certain skills and awarenesses which have relevance for writing without the child being involved with writing. This awareness opened up many possibilities to teachers. It meant that other ongoing classroom activities could contribute to the development of the child's writing skills.

6. THE WRITTEN LANGUAGE AS A SOURCE OF POWER

(a) A new status for writing

When teachers had discussed creative approaches to writing they had commented on how such approaches had given a new importance to the expressive elements in language, to the sensitive expression of the child's own perceptions, responses, emotions.

This had, however, led to less attention being paid to the relationship between the written language and thought processes.

Within our society there is a close relationship between the written language and the way in which our thinking processes are organised. The linear nature of language influences the way in which we construct an argument or demonstrate a proof. The ability of the sentence structures of writing to show the relationships between events helps us see causal relationships and to tease out generalisations from specific instances. The propositional nature of language helps us construct hypotheses, speculate, find solutions. The written language allows a more reflective approach to experience.

The more precise and organised language of writing supports thinking more effectively than the loosely organised, often imprecise, and frequently digressive language of speech.

The written language does more than give children a series of structures through which meaning may be communicated; it gives children access to a series of structures which help impose order on experiences and to find meaning in the seemingly random events of daily life.

The ability to use the written language places at the disposal of children a source of intellectual power which will influence all they do within the school curriculum. The power does not lie in the information carried by the language; it lies in the very nature of the language itself.

Of course this does not mean that children who cannot use the written language cannot think. That is obviously not so.

It does mean that children who can use the written form of language, in speech as well as in writing, have at their disposal a series of structures and relationships which help them to find meanings in a variety of circumstances and to communicate these findings economically and precisely to others.

In addition the permanent nature of writing allows the child to work on first impressions, observations, thoughts or proofs in a way which is less possible in speech. The written record allows the child to say: 'This is what I know. This is what I believe. This is what I understand.'

The child can work on present understandings to create new understandings.

This is true learning.

There were a number of awarenesses developed within the Project which were seen by teachers to be of special significance. This was one of them. At the various meetings at which teachers brought together what they had learned through working within the Project this awareness of the relationship between the written language and thought was considered by many to be the most important.

It represented not just a new understanding – for many it was a source of excitement because of the impact that it had on practically everything they did in the classroom.

As a P2 teacher said, quite simply: "It brought a new dimension to my work."

This awareness led teachers to see that there had been a serious underestimating of the ability of the young children with whom they had worked.

There were frequent comments –

"I wouldn't have asked them to do that a year ago."

"I wouldn't have expected them to be able to do that."

As teachers worked with their children they appreciated that when you teach writing as something more than secretarial skills you teach much more than writing.

(b) Writing and cognitive development
If a child produces a piece of writing which is sensitively written, appropriate to the situation and which communicates clearly and vividly, this piece of writing is not simply a demonstration of the child's language skills; it is a demonstration of all that that child is.

In trying to identify markers for the child's development in writing the project did not select purely linguistic markers.

Once again the Project turned to the meanings that children found in the experiences they were writing about. These meanings depended on a number of aspects of the child, from sensitivity through to social experience, but they were most directly related to the child's cognitive ability.

In the following examples of children's writing there has been a deliberate omission of information about the context within which the writing was produced. This will be discussed elsewhere. Readers are asked to consider how children coped with the expression of certain experiences through writing and not see these pieces simply as stories.

Three markers seemed useful:

(i) the ability of the child to hold together ideas within the sentence

As will be seen later, the work of the Project involved children in discussion about causes, purposes, consequences, etc. and one could see in the child's use of the sentence a movement from time clauses, through reason and purpose, through the occasional adversative clause where the child was able to hold contrasting points of view or to express possibilities; this is not so much a linguistic development as an intellectual one.

In the first group readers might reflect on the quite complex sentence structures which young children can employ and children's ability to handle speculation.

Holding ideas together in a sentence

P1. Yesterday my mum tripped over a black and white cat that had crept into the kitchen. The teapot she was carrying broke and the tea spilled on the floor.

P2. Jim climbed on to the box and looked into Mrs Jones' kitchen. He was so worried because no one answered the door but where was Mrs Jones? He could not find her. Maybe she was dead in the house. Jim was very worried. He kept knocking at the letter box but still no one answered the door. He went to the next house and asked if they knew what was wrong with Mrs Jones. The lady said, "Mrs Jones was having a cup of tea with me." Jim was not worried anymore.

P3. Extract.
. . . They were still talking when it started to rain. She was getting wet but she thought it was rude to say, "I must go", so that is how she got the flue. she is still in bed.

Anticipating future possibility

P2. I would not like Jimmy Crankie to come to my Christmas party because he would hit people, be bad and be sick. If he came to my party I would tell him to go away and mind his own business.

P3. If I could choose any pet I wanted I would choose a rabbit. It would have a twitchy nose and feel furry all over. Its fur might be brown and it would have a soft fluffy tail. Dad would make a hutch to keep it in. I'd give it carrots, lettuce and water and keep it away from dogs in case they killed it. In the summer I'd let it go out in the garden but I'd have to keep an eye on her in case she ran away. I would let her run around the grass and teach her to stand on her front legs.

(ii) the nature of the stance which the child held to the experience

The concept of stances has been developed in "Hand in your Writing"; in which the stances used were related to the concept of "decentering" i.e. the child's movement away from a self-centred narration of events to some awareness of the significance of the events or the seeing of the events from the point of view of another person.

In the following selection readers might consider each child's ability to do more than simply say what happened and their ability to look at experience through other eyes.

Stances: children look at their own lives and through others' eyes

P2. I remember when Mrs. M..... said "Play-time!" in a loud voice. I didn't know what play-time meant. Just as I thought this I was caught up in a crowd of children and I was bumped to the coats. I copied the other children because I thought they were doing the right thing. Now I knew what playtime meant.

P2. The old lady sat by her window and saw the fireworks display at the other end of the village. She felt sad because when she was a little girl one of her friends had a bad accident with fireworks and was blind for the rest of her life. As she watched the rockets go wurly turly up into the sky she hoped that no one would get hurt with any of the fireworks.

P3. One day I had just finished tidying up the Grant Park, when I saw two children holding an ice-lolly each. When they took the wrapper off they just dropped it. I was very angry with them because I had just finished tidying up the park. I was very tired and I wanted them to come back and pick up the rubbish themselves. I had to keep bending up and down, up and down over and over again. I wished I was at home watching television but I wasn't. I was at the park doing my duty tidying up. The children were very naughty throwing rubbish on the ground especially when I had just finished tidying the park. I gave the children a row and told them not to do it again. To let them know how I felt I told them to come back the next day to collect the rubbish. They did that and they never dropped litter in the park again.

(iii) the nature of the shape which the child imposed on the events

Much of the children's writing was in simple chronological sequence; children began to use the "three-part" sequence; the report; and some were able to deal with non-chronological shapes, as in describing a static scene.

In this selection readers might consider how children can employ chronological sequence for various purposes and this ability to use non-chronological structures to deal with material that is not telling a story.

Shapes: chronological (based on narrative) and logical (spatial)

Chronological order

P1. The naughty girl threw stones at the duck and her ducklings while they swam on the pond. The park keeper shouted at her and she ran way calling him names.

P2. Buy a toothbrush and some tooth paste. Put some toothpaste on the toothbrush and then put the toothbrush under a cold tap. Then put it in your mouth and go round and round then up and down in your mouth with the toothbrush. Then spit the toothpaste out then get a cup and fill it with water and swirl it round and round in your mouth and spit it out. Then get a towel and dry your mouth. Then put the towel back.

Three-part stories: precipitating event: main event: outcome/resolution

P1. I tripped over a lot of stones at the harbour and hurt my knee. My Mum had to put a plaster on it.

P2. The broken pieces were everywhere. I had broken a plate. I was meant to be washing up the dishes for my Mum because she was ill in bed, but I wanted to play with the plates instead. I was rolling them across the carpet when one crashed into the drawers. It made a tinkling sound when it crashed. I tried to hide the little pieces of the plate but there was nowhere to hide them.

P3. One Sunday Poochey was playing with a hose in the garden. Poochey's mum and dad told him to water the flowers because it hadn't been raining for a long time and they were dying. the hose split and . . . Splash! the water went flying all over him. He looked like a soaking wet fisherman. He had water dripping everywhere, even from his nose. He went inside to get changed and his mum laughed and laughed, and she said, 'what a silly silly boy!'

Reports: (still based on time-sequence+intention+conclusions)

P2. We wanted to find out how water got up in the air. The teacher took us to the staffroom to find out where water comes from. Miss . . . put on the kettle. We all watched the water boiling. When the kettle was boiling we saw steam. The teacher explained that we should not touch it because it was dangerous. Then the teacher got a plate from the cupboard and put it in front of the steam. It dripped with water because the steam touched the cold plate. Steam looks like clouds. Clouds have to go over somewhere cold and then it rains.

P3. In class today we tried to find out how many of each different containers we needed to fill a baby's bath. We used a long tube, a basin, a bucket and a cup. We needed 40 long tubes of water, 4 basins of water, 53 cups of water and one-and-a-half buckets of water. The basin and the buckets were the best at filling the bath because they held the most water. The cup and the long tube were the least suitable because they held the least water. when we tried to carry a full baby's bath the water looked as if it was the sea in a storm and a little splashed on the ground.

Non-chronological shapes; (based on movement through space; top/bottom; back/front)

P3. I see in the picture a boy and a girl and a snowman. The girl is wearing a pair of wellingtons, an anorak and trousers and the boy is wearing the same. The snowman is wearing a cap a brown and white checked scarf a button nose and a pair of glasses. The snowman has a spade and the ground is covered with snow and leaves. In the background there is a house the windows have blinds. The house is brick and there are plants growing up the wall.

P3. A builder has to make a house waterproof.

1. He makes the roof triangle so that water can't get in. The rain has to run down the roof.

2. He has to put on tiles so that the water cannot get into the cracks.

3. He has to put on the gutters on the bottom of the roof so that the water does not go down the wall.

4. He needs to fix drain pipes to the walls to take away the rain from the gutters.

5. He has to put a drain at the bottom of the pipes to take the water away from the house.

Although all children will show this development in their ability to express the relationship between events, to see significances in events and to impose order on their experiences, these will develop at different rates. It is possible that these developments, as indicated by the above markers, may not appear in children's writing. The examination of a large sample of children's writing that preceded "Hand in your Writing" indicated that much writing from P6 and P7 consisted of superficial and uninvolved writing which was little more than the simple narration of events in time and without those "markers" discussed above. In many cases the writing was less complex than that produced by younger children within the Project.

Had teachers spoken to the children who produced these pieces discussed in "Hand in your Writing" it is highly likely that they would have found that children could have said much more than they chose to say in their writing.

Why is this so?

(i) As described above in 5(a) the child has no audience to draw out his/her awarenesses of an experience.

(ii) If the teacher's response to the writing draws attention largely to neatness and correctness the child may pay less attention to the content.

Teachers, like Doctor Frankenstein, can create their own monsters.

In Mary Shelley's novel or in Boris Karloff's memorable portrayal of the Monster there is in that sad creature much sensitivity and a capacity for love. These admirable qualities were frustrated by an unthinking response to the appearance of the creature.

If the teacher's response is to the "appearance" of a child's writing then there is likely to be a similar frustrating of admirable possibilities – the quality of the meanings expressed and the precision of their communication.

(iii) In contrast, much of the discussion between project teachers and children about the children's experiences had to do with motivation, purpose, consequences, responses of others. In such discussion the children drew naturally on their latent language ability, especially the ability to show the relationship between events. When children wrote, project teachers would comment favourably on the economy or precision with which children held ideas together. Some teachers from P2 on, quite explicitly would put children's writing on display with their own written comments beside it drawing other children's attention to specific instances of effective writing.

Children should be in no doubt about what teachers admire and value in writing. If this is done the capacity that children show in speech should find expression in writing.

To take an example, children in P2 and later might find starting points for writing in picture-cards or pictures which teachers had taken from magazines. These might show children involved in situations in which others participated. In their discussion of such situations or in their writing on them children were encouraged to consider how the situation might appear from someone else's point of view or were encouraged to express, not just the events that had taken place, but *their own response to these events*.

In this way, and it is only one way, the child's decentring himself from involvement in the events was encouraged and became another way in which children could relate to experience.

Teachers discussed within the writing group, especially from P2 on, how the experience that the children wanted to communicate might be handled. What would the readers have to be told? Would they be able to follow and understand what it was the children were communicating?

These discussions were often extensive and demanding but through them the children began to build up a repertoire of shapes through which meaning and order could be imposed on experience so that they were more readily accessible to both the child and to her/his potential audience. These shapes did not just help the child to organise past experience; they provided "windows" through which the child could view current experience and find sense in it.

The discussion of how experiences might be organised and communicated may be more important for the development of writing competence than a discussion designed solely to stimulate the child to write.

If children are to become more effective writers then they have to become more self-conscious about their writing and more aware of what goes on when one writes. This can begin in P1, as we shall see, with the children's incorporation of significant details in writing and putting what they have to say in a simple sequence that readers can follow.

An awareness of those phases of development through which children move enables the teacher to set up situations or contexts which allow them to use their language awarenesses and skills and through use to consolidate them.

To sit back and expect these "markers" to appear in the child's writing is to see writing as a "gift", something outwith the control of the teacher.

If children develop a repertoire of structures, stances and shapes then it is easier for them to impose order on experiences.

If the children in the last two examples on p.22 had not been able to organise what they had to say from top to bottom or front to back then their descriptions/explanation would have been incoherent and the reader would learn little from them. This is another example of how a writing skill supports thought and helps the child find meanings. The extending of this repertoire of shapes continues into upper primary and secondary with shapes which are logical rather than chronological.

These markers were not used for assessment. An awareness of them helped teachers to identify where children were and this allowed the teachers to incorporate in the various contexts, writing possibilities which allowed children to use the skills and awarenesses they have developed and encouraged them to take a step forward into new and deeper understanding.

Towards the end of P3 teachers were setting up situations which encouraged speculation and problem-solving, either in "What would you do if . . .?" situations or by involving children with real life or fantasy situations which presented problems. Children were also presented with situations that required that they relate to them through the eyes of another person. There were also situations which required non-chronological organisation, like reporting back on static situations.

It would be improper to claim outstanding success in these areas. Obviously children were better in a speech situation; the problems posed by the sheer act of writing had not been completely overcome by all children.

This was a new area for all those engaged in the project. The frontiers had still to be mapped but a few hardy pioneers struggled though. There was still a tendency amongst a number of teachers to see learning to write as something that went on essentially within story-telling and there was some reluctance to teach writing through letting children use writing.

Because the markers relate more to thinking than to writing they gave the teachers an awareness of the child's ability throughout a wide variety of tasks and situations.

7. A BASIS FOR TEACHING WRITING

We started by looking at one approach to the teaching of writing and examined its weaknesses. We attempted to identify some of the things that children needed to know about writing.

Now we look at those new awarenesses about the teaching of writing on which teachers began to develop their classroom strategies.

All "writing" activities were organised within groups.

(a) building on what children already knew:
There was a growing awareness of the danger of setting up failure situations for children by involving them with writing situations which were beyond the ability of the child to employ the structures, stances or shapes appropriate to them. Teachers were more aware of what children brought to the writing task – their awareness of the written word, their understanding of story and their limited ability to appreciate the needs of their audience.

(b) differences between talk and writing:
Project teachers felt this to be an important awareness. Teachers now had the insights to engage more helpfully with children or to respond to their writing so that children began to employ the characteristics of writing, particularly its explicitness and coherence and to use the reflective possibilities of writing through redrafting.

(c) writing is not a unique activity:
The realisation that writing shared many elements with other expressive activities allowed teachers to develop skills relevant to writing away from the act of writing; this enabled teachers to anticipate many writing difficulties and gave a more coherent feel to the work of the classroom.

(d) learning writing through use:
Many teachers saw writing as a one-off activity. Children wrote their stories and these might exist quite separate from the work of the classroom. Using writing helped give children a sense of purpose and the need to consider how that purpose might be met encouraged children to consider more closely what they did in writing.

(e) writing as a public activity:
Another important awareness which had a significant effect on how teachers organised the teaching of writing.

Children now wrote within supporting, co-operative and critical groups. By working in this way each individual within the group had as a resource for learning to write: those awarenesses about writing possessed by themselves, those possessed by others in the group, those possessed by the teacher, as well as the examples offered by adult authors.

(f) the written language and intellectual functioning:
The awareness of the relationship between these two was for many teachers the most important product of their work within the Project. It encouraged teachers to look at what children wrote in a new way, encouraged the setting up of writing tasks which were far removed from the simple narratives described in "Hand in your Writing". It led teachers to a new evaluation of the ability of young children and of the status of writing within the school curriculum.

(g) the teacher's role
Creative writing had placed considerable importance on the stimulating of a child to write and on the evaluation of the child's writing once it was completed.

The various situations and contexts for writing which Project teachers provided lessened the need for more explicit stimulating of children to write. Teachers now saw their principal role as working with children on the production of writing. Children understood little of the processes of writing and it was here that teachers felt they could be of most use.

The teacher's role is such an important factor in the teaching of writing that we now examine it in greater detail.

8. THE TEACHER'S ROLE IN THE DEVELOPMENT OF WRITING

Although the children's writing tasks vary throughout the development of writing the teacher's response to the child does not. The teacher's role in the early activities was essentially to demonstrate technique, as later she would demonstrate techniques when children wrote; it was not her role to stimulate the child's production of a particular representation; the teacher might show how models could be built up using Project material, how various effects could be produced using plasticine, how backgrounds and figures could be built up using a metal board and magnetic strip.

Young children find it difficult at times to draw on their recollections and the teacher might help them in this. The various neutral backgrounds might remind children of activities that had taken place within them: stories and anecdotes might spark off remembrance; role playing and mime might call into being a child's recollections of how people behaved and of the details of physical action. The teacher has to hold back from simply making children the illustrators of her stories. Too long a discussion and the stories and recollection of the teacher or the more articulate children might dominate.

The teacher would check that all children had something they wanted to represent and then leave them. Teachers would go off to work with another group and then return to the first group to hear children's reports or the stories they had made up.

Let us look at some other aspect of the teacher's role

(i) Scribing:

When a teacher showed a visitor a story which a child had dictated she might say to the visitor: 'This is one of John's stories. He can't write it down yet.'

Gradually, the idea became accepted that this was a negative way of expressing the situation. The child who asked the teacher to scribe a story was indicating that s/he appreciated that writing was an appropriate way of recording and communicating something s/he wanted to say. This child was indicating that s/he had some idea of what writing can do.

The teacher's scribing with the child watching and commenting gave the child an excellent opportunity to see what people actually do when they write. S/he was learning something about the process of writing. S/he was also learning that something s/he said could be written down and could be read by any one, at any time and in any place – and in the exact words s/he had used. Even when the child had forgotten the story, there was still the written record.

Scribing takes time but was felt to be worth it because of the pleasure it gave children to have their stories recorded and made available to others and because the teacher and child meeting in the act of dictating/ scribing allowed the teacher to introduce the child to how one sets about writing. The teacher's role is not simply to write down what the child says but to suggest to the child that there are certain forms expected in writing. For example, the child may use the present tense which is difficult to sustain, and ignore the fact that certain information is not available to the reader.

Even after children could write, scribing was still felt to be useful. It helped children get over that frustration they feel when their need to tell stories is inhibited by a low level of writing skills and because the composing of stories in a form appropriate to writing is more important than writing the story down.

Some of the most impressive writing in the Project came from groups of children working together for several days on stories which they then dictated to the teacher.

It is also more helpful to the child to work on the same story for several days than to write a different story each day. The child must learn more by using the possibility that writing offers to expand and refine than by writing a number of stories, possibly of the same kind.

(ii) Organisation:
All "writing" activities were organised within groups. Groups could come together for various purposes but as children moved into the learning of handwriting skills a writing group was formed which stayed together; a definite area of the classroom was established as a writing corner or table and furnished and decorated accordingly; writing groups went there to do their writing.

These groups gave children some of the support they derived from other participants in conversations. Children were encouraged to discuss their work, to show and share the finished products and to criticise the work of others, particularly from the point of view of comprehensibility.

Although the Project accepted the desirability of individualised learning the numbers in the Project classes, many of which were composite, made such learning difficult. Teachers could not work all the time in a one-to-one situation. When the teacher returned to the "writing" group she might choose to work with one child with the rest of the group listening in and making comments. In work with one child the teacher shares her expectations with the whole group and in this way the children began to build up criteria for the writing of stories.

Teachers said that children did in fact build up criteria. They might criticise other children for missing out what were considered to be significant details. Teachers reported on children criticising visiting speakers for not giving enough information and one P2 class objected to a new reading book which used a number of simple sentences, saying that was not the way they wrote and offering alternative sentence structures.

Children working in a group and listening in to discussions between the teacher and individual children showed by their comments on the writing of others that they had built up criteria relevant to writing.

(iii) Teacher-response:
The Project examined the total writing output of a number of P1 classes. The comments written in the writing jotter were usually generalised encouragement of the "good work!" kind or else they referred to the formation of letters and general neatness.

It is unlikely that children would know why their work merited such approval and comments on letter formation and neatness would not help them understand the process of writing or what their readers would expect from them when they wrote.

The response made to the work produced by the P1 children within the Project was designed to encourage them to communicate with others but it was also designed to encourage children to incorporate writing characteristics in the stories they told. While recognising the important contribution made by creative writing approaches it will be appreciated that the emphasis in the Project has been on clarity in communication and coherence in ideas.

What do we mean by "writing characteristics"?

We have already said that children when they talked received a great deal of support from the context within which the talk occurred. The listener projects his/her meanings into what the speaker says. If the speaker says that a party was "great" the listener knows from his/her own experience of parties what makes one "great". If there is any doubt the listeners can always ask.

Within talk the speaker may give the minimum of information and expect listeners to expand this from their own experience.

Writing cannot count on that kind of support. The writer has to incorporate in his writing sufficient information for the piece of writing to have meaning without reference to anything else.

Talk is often digressive and repetitive. The child is improving as s/he talks and has to cope with comments from others.

Such a digressive form of communication would be intolerable in writing.

It is more difficult for most people to read something than to listen to it and readers would be unwilling to persevere with a written communication that was incoherent.

When we talk of children's talk incorporating written characteristics we mean that what the child says should have sufficient detail to make it comprehensible without additional questions and that it should be organised in such a way that a reader or listener can follow it.

(iv) "You know what I mean":
The examination of a large number of children's scribed or written stories suggested that they left out various types of information. Obviously they believed that their readers/listeners were aware of these things.

They might not say much about the various agents involved in the action. These **agents** were frequently "somebody" or "a man" and there was frequent use of pronouns without antecedent.

The **action** might not be located in time or place. The child launched into the action without putting it in any context.

Children seemed to assume that their readers would know what the **purpose** or reason for any action was and that they would appreciate the consequence. It is not as if children could not handle such things. To listen to their talk was to hear frequent mention of "going to do something"; doing something "because"; or that "something" would happen when they got back home.

Here we have a P1 child writing on the school sports. It's well-handled. The teacher's function is defined. There is the use of the present infinitive to define purpose and the use of the noun clause "who won". Despite this confidence we are not told the nature of the events nor are we told who "they" or "who" are.

"The teacher was standing there to see who won. After they went back into the classroom to get their coats to go home."

Once teachers developed this awareness of what children omitted in their statements they began to ask "Who? When? Where? Why? What happened then?" questions where relevant.

These began to be part of the **consistent response** teachers made to the children's work. With this went the reiteration of the fact that readers hadn't shared in the child's experience and if s/he wanted them to understand then s/he would have to tell them more.

Teachers knew that children had internalised these awarenesses of writing when they began to comment on other children's work within their group using these criteria.

In order to limit the amount of time spent with children, teachers devised material that helped children develop this understanding. Some of the questions – "Who? When? Where?" could form the basis for wall displays, especially once children had some reading ability. Word banks could now accompany pictures of people, places and events.

The "Who?" display related more to the attributes, character, etc. – than to the naming of kinds of people – mummy, teacher, etc. Sad and smiling faces were used to draw children's attention to "response" words.

"When?" words were difficult to display. Many teachers used a clock face to indicate time while arrows pointing forward or backwards related to time words or phrases.

Children do not have to be told what to do. If communicating with other people is important to them they will work at their communicating till they are satisfied that other people are sharing with them.

The teacher's response did not say: "You should do this." It said: "I can't understand what you are trying to tell me. You will have to tell me more or put it in a different order."

(v) Unhelpful teacher response:
The comments on stories in a number of P1 jotters revealed that the teacher's response could give children a wrong idea of writing. This was most clearly seen in the writing which accompanied drawing which is a very common practice in P1 classes.

Here are several typical sentences from P1 jotters.

This is my good baby.

Gloria and her three babies are coming to school today. (Gloria is a hamster).

Robert the rabbit is sitting beside a rainbow.

I am looking at the sunflowers in the garden.

These sentences were neatly written and correctly spelled.

Why should we not be satisfied with these?

These sentences only have meaning if they can be related to something else – a drawing, or the realisation that Gloria is not a fecund parent. The teacher accepts these because she is concentrating on handwriting skills. The child learns that it doesn't really matter what is said. Project teachers sought to get children to tell stories which could stand on their own, e.g.

P1

Yesterday on my way home from the camp site I bought a stick of rock to eat by myself.

Teachers encouraged children to say things that can only be said in writing. – "Tell me something I can't find out about in your picture."

It's the difference between a drawing with the caption: **"I am washing the dishes"** – and the caption – **"I am washing the dishes because it is Mother's Day."**

Right from the beginning there has to be the assumption that the child is trying to express and communicate meaningful things and that anything should not be accepted simply because it is neat and correct.

Another instance in which young children were not being encouraged to use the possibilities of writing was when the child has written what is an interesting story with potential for development. The page would be turned by the reader with a certain anticipation, but what followed would be a completely unrelated story.

Writing is seen here as a one-off activity – after all, if the main objective is to develop handwriting skills these can be practised in any kind of writing.

Here are a few examples:

I have not to play with Ian.

One door has two snowmen.

I was playing with Ian and the door came off the car.

Linda nearly went in the water and I got her.

In conversation the listener would ask questions about what Linda was up to; what was wrong with Ian; how did the door come off the car; and so on. These children are not being encouraged to make important detail available to the readers nor are they being encouraged to return to their stories and make those simple extensions of them that would make them more meaningful. **The fact that meaning remained with the child and had not been communicated through the written word to the readers was not considered important.**

Some of the extended statements in P1 writing jotters used speech structures, i.e. a string of statements rather than elaboration within the sentence.

I like to play football. I play with my daddy. My daddy can beat me. Once I beat him lots of times.

I like to go out in my roller boots. They are red. I play up and down with my friends. I go with my friends.

There is a great deal of redundancy here because the children are not using the possibilities of the sentences to hold a number of ideas together. To allow children to believe that this kind of writing is acceptable is to lay the foundations for future inadequate writing.

It cannot be argued that this is all the children can do for the first child might say in conversation, "I like playing football with my daddy. Daddy can beat me but I beat him once." Similarly the second child could say, "I like to go out in my red disco boots."

The short, simple sentences which characterise much of the writing of young children is not just a factor of their inability to compose more complex sentences, it may also reflect the model provided by reading schemes. Despite significant improvements, the language of these schemes does not always mirror the language children use when they speak.

It would seem more desirable to encourage children to use language with some of the characteristics of the written language right from the start, even in their oral story-telling or dictated stories, rather than allow them to form the wrong idea about how writing functions.

The teacher should show that she values the writing of young children. The fact that she talks to children about their writing is the most understandable way she can demonstrate that she cares. "I like your stories but you'll have to tell me a bit more if I am going to understand and enjoy them and I won't be able to follow your story if you jumble things up."

(vi) Asking questions

The kind of question the teacher asks in response to the child's work influences what the child chooses to recall and how it is expressed in language.

A P1 class had been reading the book 'The Hungry Caterpillar.' They had drawn pictures of caterpillars and made a study of them. They were aware of the evolution of the butterfly. They wrote stories/reports on their experiences, e.g.

We saw a butterfly coming out and we were very quiet in case it flew away.

Here the child explains why he did something. The link is quite complex "*. . . in case it flew away.*"

This story came out of discussion within the writer's group. What is important was what the teacher asked of these children. When they spoke about a butterfly coming out, or an egg on a leaf, there are two types of questions the teacher might ask. One turns the child back into the experience – what colour was the egg? What did the butterfly look like? What did you feel like when you saw it?

The other question takes the child out of the incident and links it with other things – it makes it into an event. What did you do then? Why did you do this? What happens then?

Both types of questions are quite legitimate but each draws on different aspects of the child's recollection of the incident and each draws on different forms of language.

One is more concerned with response and may draw on sense impressions.

I've had a caterpillar in my hand before and it's tickly.

The other asks children to explain their actions and the children's responses draw on their ability to hold ideas together inside the sentence.

One summer an egg was on a leaf. I was very careful so that I might not get stung by the nettle.

Both types of questions may be asked but Project teachers had some preference for the second type, partly because of the growing interest in the relationship between the writing and thinking, and partly because the second question seems to encourage the child to move out into narrative and allows the child to draw on her/his awareness of story.

9. PHASES IN THE DEVELOPMENT OF WRITING

The work of the Project was not tied to specific classes at the Primary 1–3 stages. Since the work was related to individual's development, the Project work was based on a number of key phases in the development of writing. Project teachers agreed that these phases provided a useful structure because they relate more to the way in which the child learns how to write and to use writing than to linguistic development. Of course there would be children in the same class working at different phases or at different points within one phase. The material lent itself to individualised or group work and teachers found this presented few problems in classes used to working in groups.

There was no need to postpone using writing until the child had mastered writing. If a child could write down one word – s/he could use this to identify something – "cat", write down a quality of something – "big", or his/her response to something – "dirty". If the child could write down two words s/he could tell a story – "I fell", categorise things – "big/small" or "good/bad", and so on.

As soon as a child had limited mastery over writing this could be put to use. This gave writing a purpose; provided things to write about; taught the child more about how writing functions than a diet of repetitive one-off stories. It meant also that writing could be involved in other curricular activities.

PHASE ONE:

(a) The children who entered the P1 class brought with them many **possibilities**. Some had experiences at home or in playgroup or nursery school which gave them a flying start in language work; others engaged actively and cheerfully with the work of the classroom but had not these advantages; some were silent and the words had to be patiently coaxed from them.

What the Project did in Phase One was to work with what were normally seen as expressive activities – drawing, modelling, plasticine work, etc. Since all of these have products, a drawing or a model, they are also communicative activities – they say something to other people.

Teachers in the Project placed more emphasis on the communicative aspect of these activities than was formerly the case believing that this enlarged the expressive potential of the activities and increased the satisfaction they gave to the child.

The child creates her product for other people as well as for herself. This places certain responsibilities on the child.

If the activity is purely expressive then the sheer working with the materials may be enough, e.g. broad washes of colour or the kneading of plasticine. If children are involved with communication then they have to produce something that has meaning for others who have not participated in the pleasure of producing that thing.

In writing terms that would mean that the child gives sufficient detail and puts her/his statement in a comprehensible shape.

It may be argued that this concern for communication inhibits expression. Project teachers would argue that the need to communicate experiences caused children to turn into these experiences, to consider them more deeply. This meant that the product, whatever the medium, was more considered, more complex and called on a greater degree of skill. The response that others, especially the teacher, gave to this product helped the child appreciate that the school valued him/her as an individual. The school valued his/her experiences, response to them and, eventually, interpretation of them.

The child could feels s/he was contributing to the daily business of the classroom and was not simply a passive recipient.

The Project suggested that the quality of the child's expression of an experience reflected the response that others made to the child's communication.

(b) For all children the **objectives of Phase One** were the same but it might be months before some achieved them.

(i) Teachers wanted to develop the child's **pleasure in communicating** with others through a variety of media; they wanted children to feel that the recollection of their experiences or the products of their imaginings were of interest to others and gave them pleasure also. Eventually they hoped children would have a good attitude to writing.

(ii) Children liked to listen to stories; teachers sought to develop the **children's story-telling skills** by involving them with various familiar situations or activities out of which stories might grow.

(iii) Through feedback and discussions and through the reading of stories teachers sought to encourage children to incorporate some of the **characteristics of the written language** in these stories; sufficient detail to make the story comprehensible and a sequence that listeners could follow.

(iv) Teachers sought through a drawing programme to **develop motor skills** which would be appropriate to handwriting. Some children could already draw an acceptable human figure; others produced scribbles.

(c) **The teaching of writing started almost from Day One.** Of course the children could not write but they brought with them a range of communicative techniques, some of which employed awarenesses and skills relevant to writing. Most of these communicative techniques were already present in the classroom, largely as individual activities.

The Project concentrated on activities which had certain characteristics.

(i) Children had to possess these skills already; the teacher should not have to teach them.

(ii) The activities should involve the child for a reasonable amount of time. This was not just to release the Pied Pipers for their reading practice, although it did help answer the recurring question: "What can we do with them if they aren't allowed to copy from the board?"

When children were writing for themselves we believed that they learned more from working with one piece over several drafts. We also believe that a child will learn more by a close involvement with an activity. Such involvement allows for reflection on what is being expressed and the refinement of the expression of it. The child develops good work habits, especially the ability to work without continuing supervision.

What children had to say or what they chose to represent had to be seen to be important.

What children did, had to be regarded as serious work – as serious as reading or number work, and it merited a considered response – not an anodyne tick, smiling face or stick-on label.

(d) How was this close involvement achieved?

It might be by creating possibilities within the activity for a more considered recall of experiences by children or the building-up of their imaginings. In plasticine work the use of plasticine and other materials to build up low relief models based on various "neutral" backgrounds meant that children invested a great deal of effort, e.g. an oval shape which suggested the human face might be much enhanced by a child who saw herself preparing for a party – elaborate hairstyle, features of the face, jewellery. The face might be that of a character from a story the child has made up, a clown from the Christmas visit to the circus, a witch at Hallowe'en.

Another way was to build some simple problem into the activity. Sand-play might involve the production of a garden – not just flowers, but paths, walls, benches, people. Groups of children would work quite willingly on this for a lengthy period stimulating one another to add more details.

Nothing was lost. Children still learned about the properties and possibilities of the material with which they worked; they were perfectly free to project their own meanings into the activity.

(e) These activities should share some characteristics with writing.
(i) They should provide a permanent record.
(ii) They should communicate over time and space.
(iii) They should be capable of being modified by children in the light of the response from others or their own reflection on what had been produced.

(The willingness to revise or redraft had to be developed early and become a natural thing.)

All these activities should lead to representations, e.g drawings/models, which stimulate story-telling. Particular attention was paid to the showing and sharing of these representations and stories. They were displayed throughout the classroom and the school in the most attractive manner and audiences and viewers were actively sought.

Importantly the teacher will ensure that the story can stand on its own without a need to refer to anything else.

Writing has to carry its information within itself. It has to be more than a caption to a drawing.

If the child wishes, the teacher may scribe the story. Telling the teacher what has to be written down and seeing the teacher involved in writing gives the child some understanding of the writing process.

The activities chosen were –
(i) **drawing:** this being a form of graphic representation has many similarities with writing and this formed the core of the "writing" programme in the early months.

Drawing resembles writing in a number of significant ways, as indicated above. In drawing, as in writing, the child has to be aware of what the "reader" needs to know in order to make sense of the messages. The drawer (or writer) has first to think and select what is to be shown, then include significant detail to make the message clear.

The drawing of young children is usually seen as an expressive activity but drawing records and communicates the products of the child's recollection and imaginings. Here, again, the Project emphasised the response the child's drawing won from it's "readers". The response might require that children might have to think again about the event being represented and they might have to select and incorporate significant details that would make the drawing more meaningful for the "reader".

The child was not told what to include in the drawing; the "readers" simply indicated that the meaning was unclear. It was up to the child to "redraft" the drawing if communicating was important.

This did not inhibit the child's expression through drawing. In fact, it intensified the effectiveness of the expression as children reflected on the experience being represented and had to cope with the expressing and communicating of it.

Children were eager to draw and the obvious and often rapid development in their drawing skills was a source of pleasure and pride to them and much valued by their teachers. The vigorous and detailed black-and-white drawing produced by the children were a distinctive feature of all Project classrooms.

As with other activities in this phase children were encouraged to tell the stories contained within their drawings.

These stories were not simply descriptions of the drawings. They dealt with aspects of the experience, like motivation, response, consequence, which the drawings could not represent.

Again, these stories might be scribed.

The children used a writing instrument that makes a clear line easily such as a soft pencil or a biro or felt pen. Instruments that have a triangular hold are useful because this shape encourages the correct grip, thumb and two fingers, one to each side of the triangle.

The children are not left to "draw whatever you like". Drawing is a regular and serious activity with the teacher reminding groups of children of experiences common to them all and then encouraging them to show their particular version of that experience to be "read" by the teacher. Gradually, this approach enables the children to concentrate for longer and helps them to gain the control that handwriting requires. Suprisingly, although this method appears to be natural and unhurried, it has been shown to be faster than any other in achieving this end. It is also the best way of determining when a child is ready to begin to learn how to form letters.

These children have formed all the main shapes for our alphabet in their drawings and have shown that they can place shapes accurately within shapes and are therefore ready to begin writing,

whereas these children, although able to show meaning in their drawings, have insufficient control to begin formal writing practice

Children are asked not to begin to form letters until their drawings show sufficient control.

If they are unable to control the placing of detail which is significant to them in their own drawings, they will certainly not be able to make accurately, the arbitrary shapes of our alphabet.

All copying of letters should be banned until children learn to make them properly.

Of course, the children will be at different stages in drawing and are best grouped according to the maturity shown in their drawings. For example, children who are still making scribbles would be one group:

Children who make basic human symbols would be another group:

While another would be children who can make quite clear human symbols:

Children who are not yet beyond the stage of making scribbles require special attention. Although their scribbles tend to be based on lines that represent movement the children may be unaware that such lines can be "read" and be used for communication. To draw their attention to

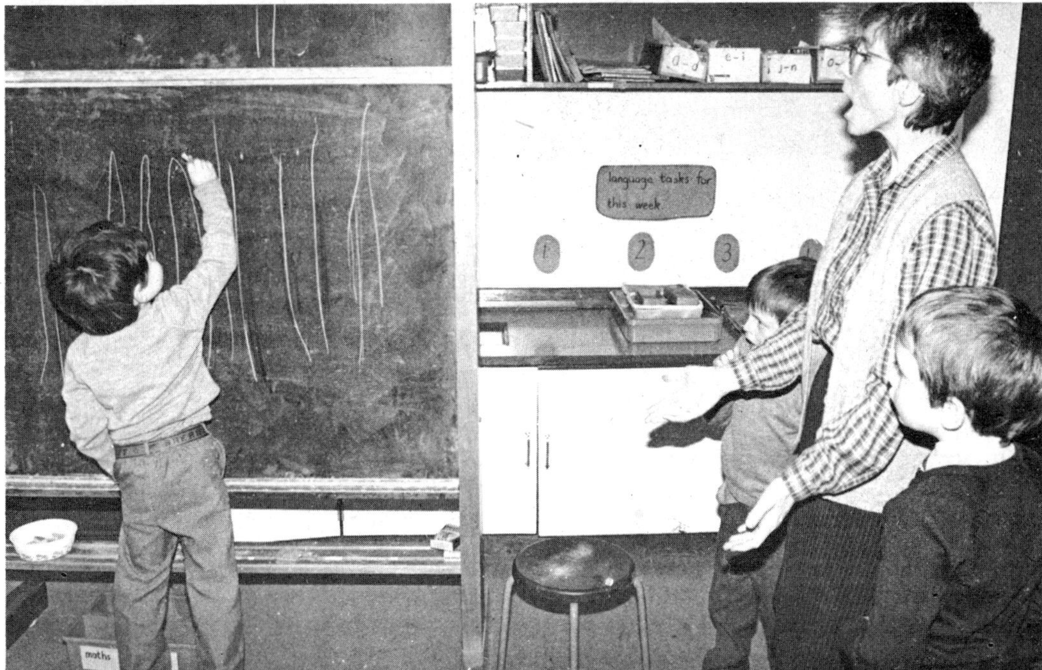

the possibility of telling stories by means of "movement" lines, the teacher can begin by inviting the children to jump up and down while holding a piece of chalk against the blackboard to show the trace of the jump or, again, drag a stick to which has been taped a piece of chalk along the playground to show the trace of the route taken. Thereafter the children can be asked to draw lines to represent recalled movements such as:

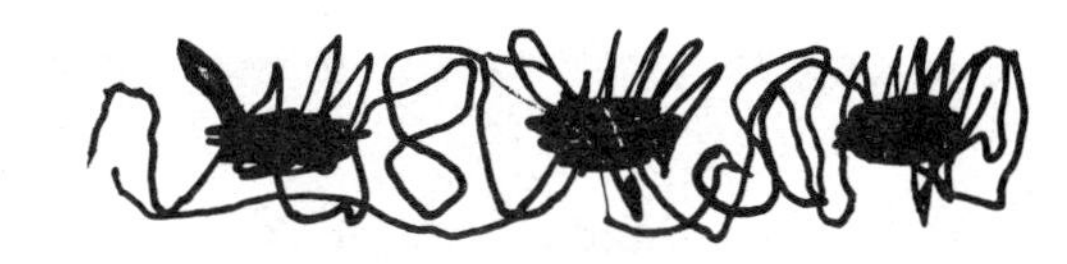

"Jumping over puddles"

or, "chasing a fly"

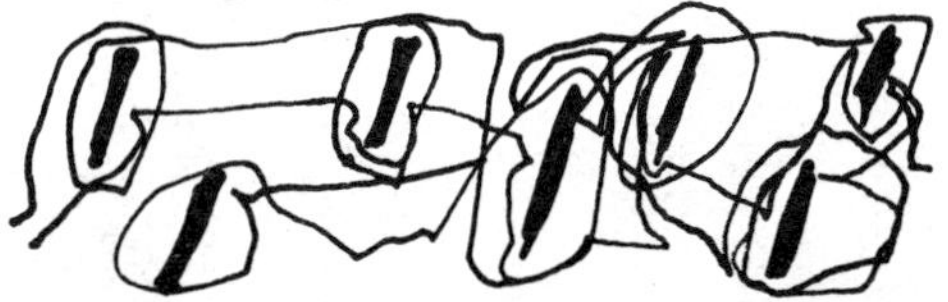

and tell increasingly complex stories such as, "chasing a friend through trees until he is caught."

Quite soon they will quite naturally move on to making symbols instead of lines because they find that the detail of their experiences cannot be represented in line alone.

The children who represent figures in symbols can be encouraged to add details such as hair or hands not by direct instruction but by reminding them of experiences that are concerned with hair or hands.

Drawings about "having tuggy hair" or perhaps "sticky fingers" can be begun by the teacher and the group acting out the experience. The teacher can then encourage them to begin with a drawing of themselves engaged in the experience they had just acted.

I have tuggy hair . . .

and a stripey jersey, trousers and shoes. After adding this detail they stop for the day.

and my mum is helping me. Finally on the second day they add details of their surroundings.

In this way, children become used to the idea that drawing (or writing) is not a "one off" activity but can be improved and revised. Quite often children will add "pseudo writing" to their pictures. This is quite different from the copying of letters and shows that they are beginning to be aware of the possibilities of writing.

Throughout, the teacher should show by her attitude that drawing is "work" and is taken seriously by her. Children need regular opportunities to draw and subjects chosen that encourage them to develop their own individual stories as in these pictures which began with the teacher reminding them of a simple action, that of bending down to reach something on the ground. Children will put this into a situation which they recall and this ensures individual results.

Although the start was the same for all the children, each remembered a different kind of incident.

Most children in the group began by showing themselves looking rather like this (which is their method of showing a person bending down).

The child on the second day made the scene into a seaside one where he was patting sand.

But this child made his picture into a description of helping his mother to pick up pins that had dropped.

Whereas this child showed herself bending down to make snowballs.

There are two related areas of teaching that will improve both the children's ability to draw more expressively and their awareness of some aspects of the writing process. The first is consistent encouragement to add more significant detail to their figure drawings (such as the pattern of clothes or hair). This helps them to concentrate for longer and see that the "reader" will find the drawing (or writing) more interesting if it contains information that will catch the reader's attention. The second is the encouragement to recall and record incidents that will tell a story. Such stories can be drawn over two or three days. The first day is devoted to drawing carefully a figure engaged in an action, while the subsequent days are used to add items that expand the picture-story. Such work helps children anticipate that a piece of writing need not be completed at one sitting, but can be expanded and improved on other occasions.

In these drawings the children began on the first day by making their figures on one side of a folded piece of paper. On the second day the paper was opened out and they enlarged their picture stories.

"Bringing home the shopping . . .

and helping Mum to put it away."

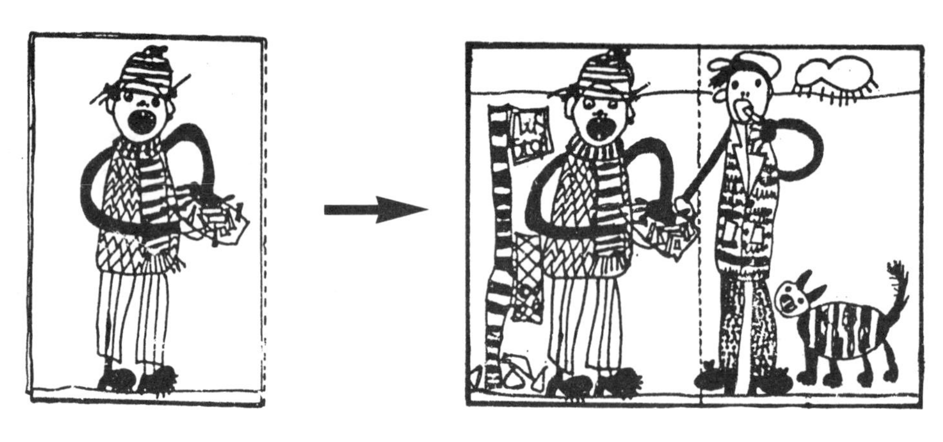

"Eating a poke of chips . . .

and sharing it with a friend (and his dog)."

"Ready for bed . . .

with all the things in my bedroom (which should be tidied)."

By means of drawing, children should be able to greatly improve their motor control, but more importantly, gain insights relevant to the process of writing in a quite natural and unforced way.

(ii) **line-work:**
The child can use three forms of graphic representation:

the **drawing** which is a moment frozen in time but can be given movement by a sequence of drawings;

the **line** which is a movement through space, and by implication, time;

the **word** which may be anywhere in time and space – drawing/line/word.

The Project encouraged the use of the line because of its capacity for recording past movement or presenting imagined movement.

Children might use the line to represent an awareness of their own movement – jumping up and down, swinging, sliding, running in circles. It could also be used to represent a route – a dog chasing a rabbit across a field, a teacher moving about a room, children coming to school, children working with apparatus in the gym. The use of the line is also described in the discussion of the Phase Two of the Project.

Children who have difficulty in seeing the line as representing movement through space may be helped by leaving a physical trace.

Their attention may also be drawn to things in their environment where lines indicate movement – jet-trails in the sky; lines of footsteps in the snow or in the sand; dirty paw-marks across a floor.

The teacher may involve them in activities in which a line demonstrates movement – a child running across the red blaise of a playing field may drag a stick behind him leaving a trace that others may follow, etc. Line activities in the Project worked best in association with some other activity, eg using the line to record the movements of characters on a story; using lines to give movement to figures in an environment.

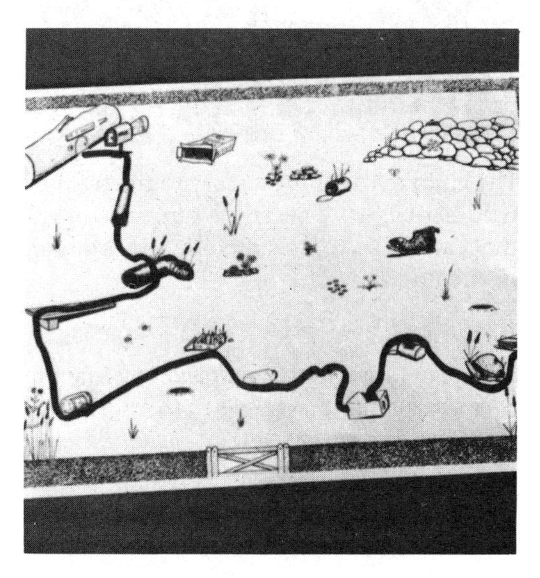

Sometimes within the Project a child might use all three forms of graphic representation to communicate a story.

A child may choose a neutral background, say a beach, and then uses drawing to create the people who will visit the beach. These are then cut-out and stuck on the background.

The child uses lines to show the movement of these characters across the beach.

The child may dictate a story to the teacher who scribes it. The story can say things that cannot be represented by the drawing or the line.

P1 (scribed)

Yesterday I went to the beach with my Mum to have a swim. I saw a big crab in the water and I was frightened. Mum said we should go home because it was too cold. I got crisps.

The story can say things about

purpose – "to have a swim";
response – "frightened";
reason – "because it was too cold";

The story can say what people thought and said.

Project teachers deliberately sought to encourage children to say through writing things that could not be said through other forms of graphic representation.

Some children also used the line as an embryonic form of writing, the line reproducing the profile of a line of script. This "writing" was often added to a drawing and represented the story of the drawing. Despite the usefulness of the line in recording movement there were some difficulties.

Some children found it difficult to grasp the symbolic nature of the line, that is that the line represented movement through space. To show movement, say of a person or animal, they would draw a series of figures as in an animated cartoon.

Generally speaking, lines were produced very quickly. Line work seemed to be most effective when associated with another activity such as figures and background or the retelling of a story. It did demand considerable teacher participation.

(iii) plasticine modelling:
The possibilities of plasticine work were improved by giving the children a "neutral" situation to enhance; children could select from a number of A4 sheets which fitted into plastic envelopes; on the sheets were printed blank faces, places familiar to the children, etc. These were "people" or enhanced by the children using plasticine and other materials. This was an extremely popular activity and led to many good stories. The children were also free to draw basic pictures which could be slipped into the envelope and enriched with plasticine additions. Teachers might make up their own basic pictures which related to some theme being investigated.

This activity helped children to concentrate and to place more meaning in the basic pictures. Unlike drawing these low-relief plasticine pictures are not a frozen movement in time as they encourage the child to add or alter so that a story can develop. It was also possible to provide a number of low-relief pictures that could be placed together so that a group of children could imagine a character (animal or human) that moved between the plasticine pictures and responded to what was represented in each.

Children enjoyed making an environment, eg a road which passed through various backgrounds. They then "walked" that road describing what they might see and making up stories about adventures that might happen.

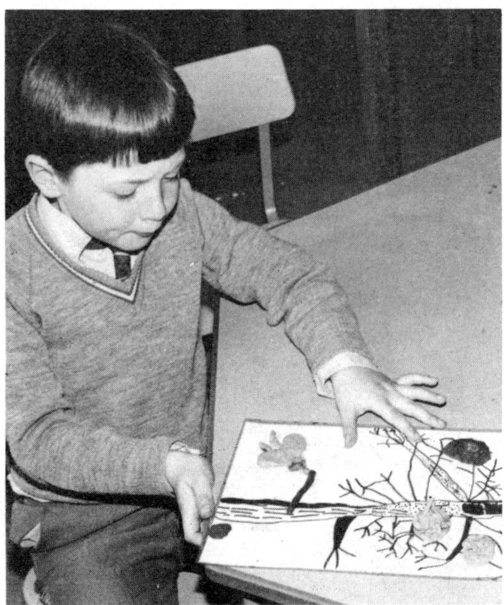

Children drawing trees and adding plasticene nests and birds.

Other groups made collaborative pictures of a rookery with nests, eggs and birds by drawing individual trees, placing them in plastic folders and adding details in plasticine.

In another group, children working on the theme "Where the Wild things Are," each contributed his/her plasticine picture to build up the island of the Wild Things.

(iv) sand-play:

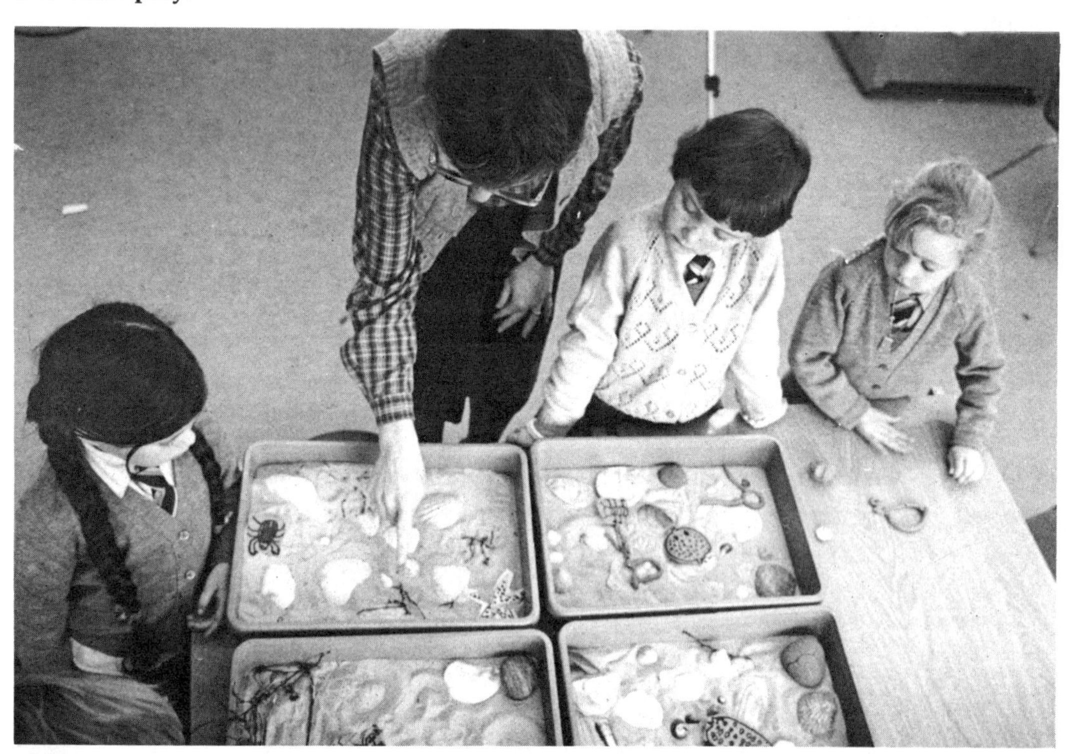

Some Project schools tried out individual sand trays; children had their own tray. This contained sand and a selection of objects, real or toy, relating to a topic, eg seashore, roadworks, farm, etc. Children could create their own worlds often from quite simple objects, acetate sheet for sea or pond, twigs for trees, small stones for rocks. Problems could be introduced – how to bridge water or protect ships from storms. These "worlds" could relate to themes which the class was investigating giving children another level of awareness. This use of sand-play was part of the Project's belief that activities should engage children for extended periods, increase their concentration span and give them opportunities for discussion, story-telling and problem-solving.

(v) constructions:
Some of the commercial construction material used in classrooms present children with too few possibilities for making models based in their own experience.

Instead of a box of indefinite pieces the teacher can organise the material to present a number of potential starting points.

For example, the provision of a wheeled base can suggest to children a number of vehicle bodies.

Similarly, the provision of a paper ladder can suggest to children a number of constructions using the ladder.

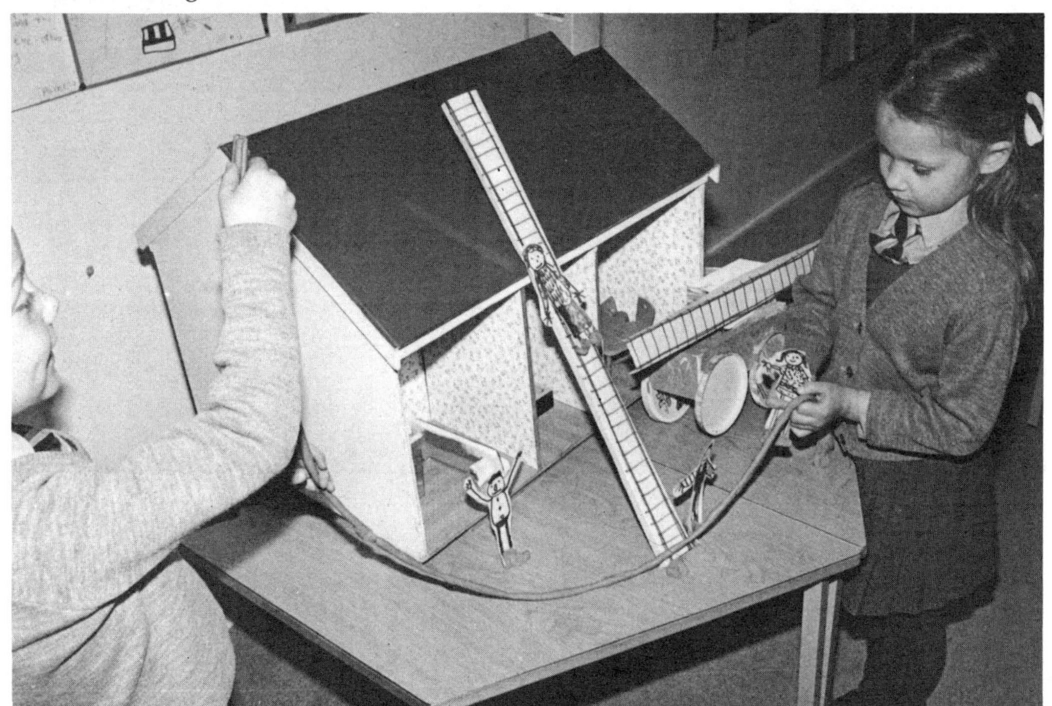

Such contructions are designed to encourage discussion and co-operative story-telling. The teacher will have to set up a situation which involves children solving a common problem, eg the building of bridges; the making of a zoo; adventure stories like the construction of an impregnable castle to ward off some enemy or quest stories in which children have to bring together creatures and vehicles to rescue someone in peril.

Children use their constructions to play out the story they can then represent through drawing or in words.

(vi) story-building:

Throughout the Project various activities called on a range of neutral backgrounds and contexts depicting places known to children; also available were a number of snap-shot figures which were again used for various purposes. Children can use these backgrounds for their own story-telling. The figures can be used to play out an incident and the children would tell this in the past tense. On other occasions they would play out another incident and tell this, always using the past tense. In this way they would make up a shaped serial story which could be scribed, recorded or written. This was so popular and successful that the range of backgrounds, figures and objects was extended to increase the range of possibilities based on the children's own experience.

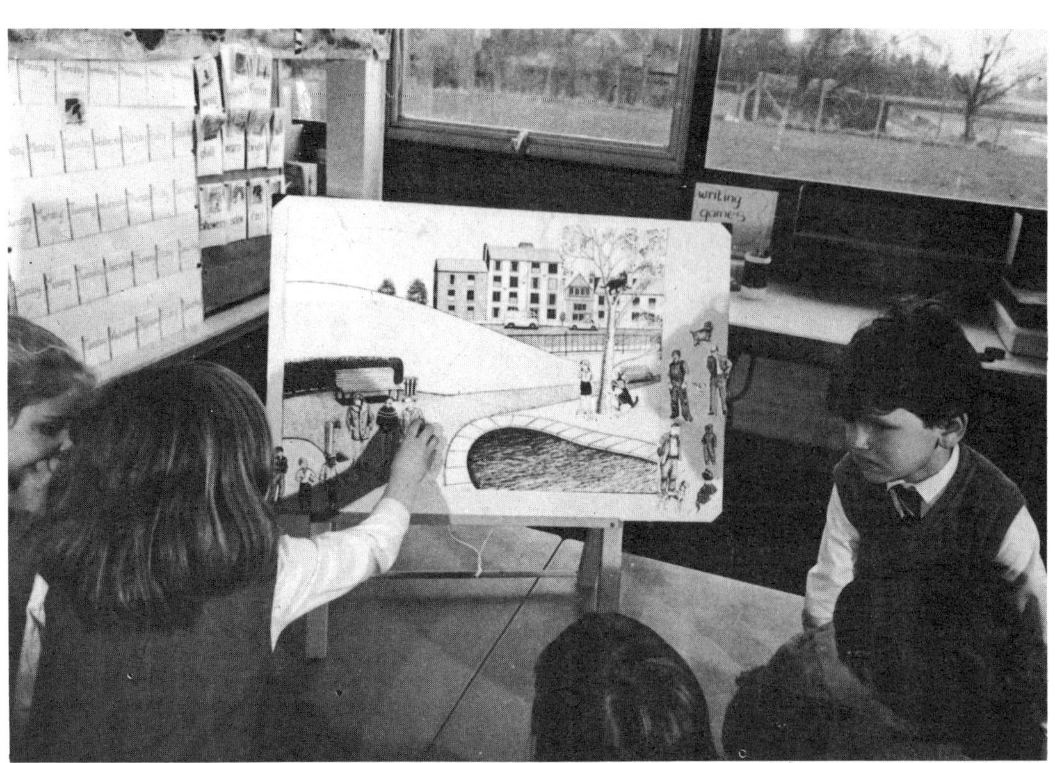

(vii) talk:

Obviously talk was the most important communicative medium; this was an essential part of all activities as children reported on what they had been doing or told stories derived from their representation.

(viii) drama:

Like talk there was no specific material for this as it might be used quite informally by teachers to support writing activities. Children used mime to help them recall the precise nature of activities. One might enter a room to find a group of children assiduously "washing" the teacher's hair before drawing their pictures or dictating their story.

Certain words like verbs and adverbs were used sparingly by children. The teacher might ask children to mime particular movements to help children build up a repertoire of action words.

Role-playing could be used to help children see experiences through the eyes of others, eg in the Bonfire Night theme one group of children might be role playing the excitement and apprehension of a group of children at a bonfire while another group might role play a nervous old lady. The groups were brought together and encouraged to interact. Out of this writing would come.

Drama is a powerful form of representation which can be used within the demands of the Project without elaborate preparation.

Children show what they can recall or imagine and in that way deepen the recall and the imagining.

PHASE TWO:

In Phase One teachers sought to encourage the children's willingness to communicate their experience and imaginings to others. Using a variety of activities teachers had developed skills and awarenesses relevant to writing and had helped each individual communicate stories in a way characteristic of writing. Through the teacher's scribing the child had learned something of the processes of writing and the drawing programme in particular had developed motor skills which would contribute to the aquisition of handwriting skills.

The work of Phase One will continue and to it will be added the work of Phase Two.

The objectives of phase Two are:

(i) Teachers sought to encourage children **to develop their narrative skills** through the retelling or composing of longer stories.

(ii) Teachers sought to develop the child's control over **story organisation** other than simple time sequence, eg the use of three-part sequence.

(iii) Teachers sought to encourage children to use **clusters of words rather than single words** in expressing their awareness of significant items in their story telling.

(iv) Teachers sought to help the child master the **formation of letter shapes**.

(a) drawing:

The various activities described in Phase One could be used to sustain longer narratives; the most effective was drawing. A child could now produce a sequence of drawings which helped support a longer narrative.

The following is a dictated story based on three pictures.

P2

One rainy day Mary was walking down the road and she met a friend. Then a dog came along and said "Woof" and scared Mary away. What a laugh she had! Mary decided to go home for her witch's hat. Her friend said, "Wait for me. I'll come and get mine too." Then they came back to look for the dog and scare him but they could not find him so they went home again. Then they went to the park and played hide and seek. Mary counted to 10 and said, "Ready or not!" Jane said "yes". When Mary found Jane she said, "Let's stop and look for the dog." They searched and searched and they found him hiding in the bushes – the very same bushes as Jane had hidden in!

The story is rather longer than the girl can handle and it shows a certain slackness. The story is also rather derivative but it gave great pleasure to writer and readers.

(b) line-drawings:
The line-drawings were used in two ways; one was with stories which were read to the children. The stories had strong narrative lines, eg a hawk chasing a mouse; Red Riding Hood escaping from a wolf. The children enjoyed the stories and they retold them using line as an aide-memoire. The line was drawn on an A4 sheet which reproduced the context of the stories. These sheets have now been redrawn so that the stories are more open-ended. The child can produce his/her own conclusion to the story.

The lines were also used with a series of neutral backgrounds known to the child – sea-shore, wasteland, park, etc. The child built up a story on the sheet using the line to record movement.

This had certain weaknesses. Children tended to say things like – "I went here then I went there and then there . . ." again supposing their listeners were aware of the detail of the story.

The stories were improved when children cut out figures representing the characters in the story and stuck them on the background. They then tended to talk in more detail about the behaviour of the characters in the story.

Here is a P1 dictated story in which the child has incorporated some of the detail which appears in the background sheet.

After dinner the girl went for a walk to the beach. She looked at the sand-castle a baby had built first and then to look for crabs. She saw three crabs on the stones. She walked down to look at the wine bottle then jumped over the water on her way home.

(c) "The Park" stories:
Another device for building up narrative control was what was called "The Park" stories. Children were read a story about the adventures of children in a park. They retold the story using a background and cut-out figures and objects. The story was retold as a group activity. Children would volunteer the next step in the story and would indicate which figures should be used: "I think it's this figure because it says she was a school girl with glasses and pigtails."

In addition to encouraging the building up of narrative it was hoped that children might pick up clusters of words which they might incorporate in their own stories.

Children used the backgrounds and figures to make up their own stories. This was extremely popular and often became an independent activity. When the children had composed their story they usually told it to the teacher who might scribe it. Some classes used listening centres and after the story had been composed the children would record it on a cassette recorder which had the controls clearly marked. Other children would listen to this recording.

In some classes this composing, recording and listening went on without any participation from the teacher.

The following is a five part sequence, partly dictated, using characters and situations from a series of Project stories about children playing in the park.

Mr Brown is having his sandwiches and Mr Jones is watering the flowers. The little dog is getting little drips from a tap.

The dog is running about barking and the cat is up a tree. The two little girls have just come into the park and they are thinking what to play.

Billy goes through the muddy puddle with his bike.

Betty is holding on to her balloon tight in case the bully boy snatches it.

The fisherman is trying to get the ball back with his rod and the girls are watching him getting the ball.

The episodic nature of this sequence interferes with coherence and comprehensibility. The reader has really to know "The Park" stories to fully understand this story.

(d) Story-books:
Children select a story-book. This is a book of some six pages which has a stated theme, eg "Jim's Bad Day". Each page will have a phrase which helps the child structure his/her story – At breakfast/On the way to school/At playtime . . . and so on. There is usually a concluding statement – "I've had a bad day", said Jim.

On each page the child will write her/his version of what happened to Jim. The book is personalised and usually heavily embellished and illustrated.

(iv) another aspect of the story book was that they could provide the teacher with indications of what interested children.

Children just learning to write enjoyed them and children who had difficulty writing found that they could produce something that others were willing to read and which gave them some pride.

Examples

The "Look" book

Look. I can swim. Look at me I can jump off the side.

These books had various purposes:

(i) they showed children how to build up a longer narrative;

(ii) certain books, eg the "Ouch" books, encouraged impression and response;

(iii) the idea of the books could be adapted to any purpose and teachers began to make up their own books some of which related to themes with which their classes were engaged;

Oh look, this policeman is arresting this man!
Oh look at this mouse squeak! squeak!
Grandad I can swing! Look! Look!

"Ugh!" book

The lady's man was getting buried and she said – Ugh! because he's a skeleton now.
I see a dead bird – Ugh!
I saw a man being sick – Ugh!

A P2 child writes in a book produced by a teacher.

In the holiday I went to the circus with my mummy because I wanted to see the animals.

I saw a hairy monkey swinging in a high trapeze and a monkey on a bike doing funny tricks.

When the cirus finished I was sad because I liked the animals and I had to go home.

(e) three part stories:
This book used the idea of the three part story. One of the aspects of writing that creates difficulty is the selecting of what will be written. There is not the same problem in talk where a child may go over what has to be said until s/he gets it right or where listeners may indicate their acceptance or not of what had been said.

It seemed that asking children to select the main incident to be written about and then asking them to consider both the cause and the outcome might give them a structure which would help in the identification and selection of significant details and might cut out redundancy.

This proved to be a structure that most children could handle, it produced writing which had a certain neatness about it and seemed not to encourage long, slackly organised pieces.

Much writing within the Project is comparatively short and the concentration throughout the Project on motivation, purpose and outcome seems to have directed some attention away from the simple narration of the events on to the consideration of human involvement in events.

The easiest way to get children using this structure is by the use of a picture or of a child's own drawing. The child says what s/he believes is happening. Obviously the child's own drawing represents his/her own story and the picture cards used by the Project present a situation for which

the child has to find an explanation. Many explanations are possible. S/he is then asked to consider the circumstances that led to it happening and the possible result or consequence.

Some teachers used a sequence of three drawings to support the story-telling or writing, as in the following. The teacher gave the title to the groups.

Interestingly, in this approach the child starts by considering the middle of the narration. This seems to have a controlling influence on what the child says or writes. When the child starts at the beginning s/he may have little ideas as to where s/he is going and the result may be a rather incoherent piece.

The child started by making a drawing of herself washing a dress. She then drew a picture of getting the dress dirty and then she drew the picture of the dress being hung up to dry. It was after the pictures had been drawn that the child wrote the story.

On Tuesday Marie fell and got mud on her red dress

Mum said she could wash it herself and put it into the machine.

When it was washed she hung it up to dry but then the rain came on.

Here the story follows the chronology of the incident.

P1 (scribed)

Hazel was getting her hair washed by her Mum.

She got nippy soap in her eyes and she was crying.

Mum dried her eyes on the towel and gave her a big kiss.

It may be that there are hierarchical differences here. In the second story the child builds up the story step by step whereas in the first story the child composes the story as a complete unit – supported by the drawings, of course.

Teachers could draw their own pictures or select pictures from various sources which related to work going on in the classroom.

P2 story – written

A Magic thing happened when I was asleep

One morning when I was sleeping my horse came out from under my snooker table and grew big.

My horse put its little saddle on and went outside to the shop and picked up a paper.

Splash! Jane has been so busy reading her new comic that she didn't see the big stone. She tripped over it and fell into the puddle of muddy water. What a mess! Jane was covered in thick gooey mud from head to foot. Jane started to cry because she was afraid that her mum would scold her. Jane ran home quickly. Her mum called her a silly girl and made her change. Then she gave her a lovely hot drink.

(f) instruction games:
Children were introduced to another activity during their audience and to encourage them to use clusters of words. This was the instruction game.

He took the paper back home. He put it down for my dad and dad got some carrots for him.

The next story had its origin in a picture of a soaking wet child. There was a brief discussion of the picture in the group. This story was written by one child within a P2 group.

Children worked in pairs; each had a copy of the same plan, diagram, picture. This could represent fields, streets, open wardrobe, clothes line, etc. The children were separated by a screen. One child had to place objects on the plan and give instructions to the other child to do the same.

I'm putting the black and white lying-down cow in the field; the field with the tractor. It's in front of the tractor.

Alternatively children might have to guide their companion. Both traced the route on acetate covering the plan.

"Start at the telephone box and go up the street to the park gates. Go into the park . . ."

After the game the children compared their plans. This was a very popular activity and one which children often chose to do. While some tasks, hanging clothes on a line – *"I'm hanging up the long-sleeved shirt with the spots"* – were comparatively easy, there was some feeling that children got more out of this activity if it was postponed until later. Also children left to themselves began to find ways of making the game easier. Teachers had to listen in from time to time to ensure that the intended precision in the use of language was maintained.

Both this game and line-work encouraged the children to use prepositional phrases. Teachers encouraged this as it helped the children place actions in time and place and provided a useful link from the verb/ action into the physical and human context in which it took place. Classrooms displayed many ingenious ways of introducing children to such words. Labels showed the relationship of objects in space. Some teachers would place a toy animal in some position in the classroom and children entering the class would have to say where "Topsy was that day" – "on top of the cupboard/under the desk", etc. This then led to stories about how the animal got there. One teacher made up board games with prepositions on the faces of the dice and movement through the game controlled by the prepositions thrown. Activities like physical education provided opportunities for introducing children to prepositions, verbs and adverbs.

Here is a P1 story by a child whose group had made a collage of autumn leaves. It is based on prepositional phrases.

"I am gliding over a tree, over a fence, through a hedge and into the gutter. A little boy stepped on me and I went crunch."

The following is a P2 story written within the "Sam the Cat" theme and following the reading of the poem: "Cats Sleep Anywhere".

"My cat sleeps beside the tumble dryer, on my lap, behind the piano, under the table, in a box, by the fire, on a cushion – my cat sleeps anywhere."

These kinds of stories were popular with less able children who could construct stories in which they could take some pride but which used limited language resources.

It should be stressed that the use of these various techniques is not dependent on the Project material.

The material is usually quite simple to make. The Project package contains material which may be used by teachers as examplars. Importantly it helps support the teacher until she begins to be aware of how the Project approach operates. Some material is, however, more difficult to produce in the classroom and the Project material is more child-proof.

Some teachers used the material as if it were a series of one-off activities. They might use half-a-dozen line-drawing sheets and then work through several instruction games. The material would then be put away. The material is not meant to be used in that way and if it were to be so used it would be ineffectual. The material is not so magical that a brief exposure to it will bring about writing competence.

The material represents a series of communicative techniques which the child may use record and express experience or imaginings in a wide variety of curricular contexts. They should not be seen as unrelated one-off actvities.

These activities draw on skills which the child finds enjoyable to employ and all of them contain elements which will contribute to later writing ability.

The fact that they are introduced during Phase One and Two does not mean that they are only used then. They can be used at any time – up to P7 if necessary.

What is important is that these techniques should be used to allow the child to express; that the teacher should be aware of their relevance to the development of writing skills; that the teacher's response should be consistent and repetitive.

Children should be building up a series of skills and awarenesses that will help them find, organise and express meanings; and a set of criteria that enable them to do this in ways which are accepted as being appropriate to writing.

Two instances of the use of Project techniques within themes

A P1 class was working with a music-based fantasy theme "The King's Diamond". The Project directors were asked to suggest ways in which language activities, especially writing activities, could be introduced into this. Various suggestions were made.

What resulted was a fine example of how the activities listed above could be incorporated in a theme. Children wrote and dictated stories, newspaper reports, descriptions, instructions. Line-work and plasticine modelling were adapted to represent incidents relating to the theme. Instruction games were employed using objects derived from the theme to build up environments relevant to it. Figures and backgrounds were used to support stories. Sequences of drawing were used. Children identified characters on the basis of descriptions given, and so on.

The full range of communicative techniques leading to language expression were used to support the fine musical element and the impressive co-operative art work within the theme.

The children were learning to use the language by using in a context which defined purposes and which proved a consistent and helpful response. The Project material was being used, as it was intended to be used, to provide a series of recording and communicative techniques and not as a fragmented series of one-off activities.

Two P2 classes in schools in the same town were working on Project themes. They were "Mr Togs" type themes – one built round a postman and the other round a shopkeeper. It was decided that the postman's baby and the shopkeeper should meet. The themes revolved round full-scale environments and figures so the shopkeeper in her magnificent hat, and lolling in a somewhat inebriated posture, was wheeled to the rendezvous. The characters met; the children had a modest repast and were involved in a series of activities – bark rubbings, collecting, observations. That afternoon one of the Project directors happened to visit one of the classes and the Assistant Headteacher suggested they should let him know what they had done. Those who could, wrote. Some produced sequences of drawings. Some used a park background with their own figures and lines. Some used a park background and enhanced this with plasticine.

Every child in the class was able to produce a permanent record of the visit to the park.

Again what had started as Project material was being used a series of techniques to record and express children's experiences.

Language games and individual expression.

It may be felt that engaging children with games or activities may stifle a child's individuality. We do not believe this to be true if the activities are used properly.

If, however, a teacher takes one of the Project activities, gives it to the whole class and prescribes what they should do and the outcomes, then there would be a denial of individuality.

We emphasise that the child's response using the the Project material should always be –

> **individual – because the Project provides a series of neutral situations and contexts**
>
> **differentiated – because, as illustrated above, the child may select topics and ways of recording and expressing these which reflect interest and present awarenesses and skills**
>
> **relevant – because the child inhabits the material with his/her meanings; and is not asked to struggle to make sense of adult concepts or adult values.**

(g) letter formation:
It is during this phase that children begin letter formation. Their readiness for this relates to their performance in drawing the human figure. Children who come together for handwriting work will form a writing group which will remain together.

> **Handwriting is a sub-skill that cannot be taught effectively unless there is a policy that embraces the whole school.**

Everyone must agree on the purpose of handwriting, on the shapes of individual letters and on the way handwriting will be taught so that pupils do not have to alter style or letter shapes when they change classes. Consistency is essential.

In many schools this policy is dictated by a commercially purchased handwriting schemes yet some of these schemes are ill-suited to produce the desired outcome, handwriting that is both fast and legible. In almost every case, commercial writing scheme books bring a poor return for money and, in some cases, actually retard the children's progress.

Choosing a writing scheme
There are two principles that govern the choice of scheme. The first is that all the letter shapes must be "writing" shapes and not "print" shapes to ensure an easy flow and rythm. For example, this is a print y and w and this is a written y and w .

The second principle is that children should begin by learning the exact letter shapes that they will maintain all the way from primary 1 until primary 7. It is quite confusing for children to begin with shapes like k which later change to k as in some writing schemes. It is also better for children to begin with letter shapes that encourage them to move freely to the next letter. If letters that have descending, finishing strokes such as

adhiklmnqt

are given a slight up-turn at the base, children will be able to increase their speed of writing earlier. This is not in order to join letters, but merely to improve flow from the outset. The ideal letters should look rather like: abcdefghijklmnopqrst uvwxyz

What is being taught?

Handwriting is only useful when it is fast and legible and when children do not have to think about how to form letters and can engage their minds totally in the composing of writing. It is a mistake to regard handwriting as a thinking process. Like a tennis player, the child should practise so that each stroke is quite instinctive leaving the mind free to decide what to do; the tennis player, perhaps, to place the ball in a baseline corner or the writer to be free to decide whether to say "tall" or "large". The kind of teaching that is required is the same for the writer and the games player.

Both must engage in a great deal of physical practice. Both must practise at the speed they will require to make the strokes. A tennis player must practise strokes at the speed of the game. The writer must practise letterforms at the speed of writing. There is no other effective method.

This means that tracing letters and careful, neat drawings of letters in copy workbooks are a waste of time, particularly when there are lines in the books because children then slow down to ensure their letters touch the lines to make them look neat. It also means that children should be discouraged from unsupervised copying of letters until they can make them instinctively and correctly.

Is there a sequence in teaching handwriting?

First, the children must have sufficient motor control to begin. This is best judged by the type of drawing they make to represent a person within determined conditions. Children who can, within their drawing, place shapes within shapes accurately, are ready to begin,

but those who have not reached that stage should have regular drawing practice.

Next, children should learn to write letters in groups of similar strokes:

coe agdq rnmhk iltf uw bp uy

This is because the repetition of similar shapes in their handwriting work for a number of consecutive days reinforces the route formation for the children.

Now comes the method of teaching the children to gain the habit of forming each letter correctly. It is essential to realise that this can only be done kinaesthetically and that writing letters at a reasonable speed is the best practice of all.

If the teacher had the time, she could supervise this work in groups, but since she does not, another method has been found. The Project discovered that the best method was to cover letters on which the correct route is indicated with acetate over which the children can draw in order to find out the "feel" of the letter route. Unlike tracing, no mark is left on the acetate and so the children draw quickly enough over the letter to aquire the feel of the stroke sequence. Thereafter they write the letter on paper, return to the acetate, write another letter and so on until they have established a movement pattern.

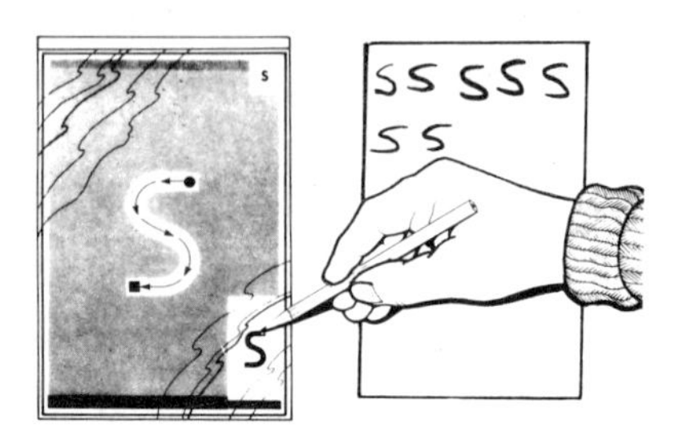

Left handed child **Right handed child**

Since the children are able to determine their own comfortable writing position, left-handed children are not disadvantage. The left-handed child slopes the card and paper to the right while the right-handed child slopes the paper and card to the left.

There are two other important types of practice to be carried out before children are able to compose without the teacher scribing for them.

The first is to combine the letters that they are learning in groups so that they become used to the appearance of written words and the spaces between words.

Small acetate covered cards can be made to provide graded groups of letters. The first group should have letters which all have the same height of start point, eg

coo coo moo moo too too raa

the next has the same height of start point, but also has ascenders

The next have descenders:

ogg ogg goo goo

then there are the ascenders and descenders:

dog dog log log log doo doo

and finally, words which have a mixture of start points like –

bow wow silly billy
boo hoo boo hoo
bad lad odd bod

The other important type of practice is for the increase of speed. Children should never compete with each other but should see if, by "training", they can increase their speed of making a number of the same letters against a ten second timer.

Writing in groups

Although, at first, it takes time to establish handwriting groups, it does allow teachers more time later for children are then able to practise on their own. This does not, however, mean that the teacher does not check their work. It is important to maintain standards from the first. It is all too easy for incorrect hand-holds to creep in or for letters to become badly shaped like this. cc

If children practise incorrect shapes too many times, these will become standard and difficult to re-teach. When bad habits have been identified, it is easy, with the use of cards, to send children to the writing table to pick out the ones they need to re-learn and this does not involve the teacher in much work.

When can we dispense with handwriting practice?

Gradually handwriting practice can be reduced, but never stopped. A handwriting practice programme can be devised to increase speed, to increase flow and to practise start point relationships as a means of helping children to write in a straight line.

The number of letters or words should be kept short and the children should be asked to repeat them at speed. In this way, they can learn the various patterns of handwriting without being diverted.

phrases like ....

bib bib bib bib

hip hop hip hop

Children should see handwriting as a pleasurable activity, free from all stress. When children acquire, as most do, incorrect habits, the important thing is not to keep asking them to change but to send them for some physical practice which will alter the habit in the same way as a games player's coach would do. It is important to remember that handwriting is a physical and not an intellectual sub-skill.

PHASE THREE

The work of the preceding phases continues into Phase Three which builds on what has been done.

By now children should be communicating willingly in words or visual representations. Oral or scribed stories should have some of the characteristics of the written language. They should contain sufficient detail to be easily understandable without reference to anything outside the story and children should be able to impose a shape on what they wish to communicate. Certain criteria should be beginning to emerge by which the child will evaluate writing, his/her own and that of others. The child's motor control is adequate to sustain handwriting skills.

Now the child moves to "real" writing.

The principal objective now is **to move the child from communicating through the spoken word to communicating through the written word**. This is a difficult and frustrating time for many children who must feel inhibited from expressing what they want to express, although the Project has anticipated this by developing many of the component skills of writing in advance of writing. What the child has been involved with up to now has been a preparation for the child working on his/her own. The Project sought to anticipate the difficulties of this moment and the needs of the child.

The child has some awareness of composing skills – purpose, finding material, language of writing, some sense of audience. The child has developed the important secretarial skills of handwriting.

The difficult choices facing the solitary writer have been replaced by the child writing within a stable group selected for their skill in drawing the human figure and remaining together to develop handwriting skills and for the composing, discussing and criticising of stories.

Teachers had been given a clear set of objectives in writing skills towards which they could work.

The child begins to write for her/himself using word-cards from a small selective vocabulary to build up stories in a **story-board**. The words chosen are not the most commonly used words, many of which have little story content, but words which children are most likely to use in story telling. Only a few nouns and adjectives are supplied because of the wide range that children compose seem to avoid the domesticity which characterises certain other schemes.

It may seem peculiar to use word-cards when the child can form letters but the use of cards further reduces the difficulties encountered by the child as he begins to write. Language is an extremely abstract subject yet, unlike in number, little concrete writing material is used in schools. The cards can actually be manipulated by teacher and pupil so that by moving the cards around some awareness of the English sentence is built up. This enables the teacher to share with the children an understanding of the written language.

The story-boards and cards allow the child to compose stories of several sentences using the normal left to right directionality. The boards can be easily stored so that the child can return to work on his story, the word cards making revision and redrafting comparatively simple. With children just beginning to write, stories have their beginning in the verb card, which is colour coded, because the action word contains the embryo of the future story.

The child is not expected to write out all the stories composed using cards, as the actual composing is more important than the writing out. The teacher will still continue scribing. Amongst other things this helps the child compensate for the restrictions that writing will place on expression. The use of scribing and other forms of communication, drawing, etc. keeps the communicating drive going during this transitional phase.

Beginning writing

(a) A teacher is working with a group of children. The teacher or a child may volunteer an anecdote about something that has happened. Perhaps a child's drawing or a plasticine picture provides the starting point. Perhaps Project material provides a context which sparks off a story.

The teacher and the children may start talking about falling down; someone has fallen down on the way to school. The teacher may decide that this writing group is ready to start composing and "writing" stories for themselves and that she will not scribe these stories for them.

With the children assisting, the teacher chooses a colour-coded word card. This is visually-cued and contains a finite verb in the past tense, e.g. "fell".

The teacher puts this word in the story-board and builds up a short story using word-cards from the word bank or writing out cards if necessary. She talks about what she is doing and encourages children to use such language skills as they possess to help make up the story, eg awareness of initial letters, length of words. Phonic skills acquired in reading or in the hand-writing kit are deployed.

She proceeds to show them how to build up a story using word-cards. She talks them through the building up of a story. She is the master-writer with her group of novices.

Commonplace verbs like "fell" contain many stories waiting to get out. Verbs in the Project kit are of this kind. They are not linking verbs, eg "was" or "domestic" verbs like "shop". Word cards on "domestic" themes like "going shopping" were tested in the first year of the Project but quickly adandoned as these topics did not lend themselves to the development of a story. Children found little memorable in such topics.

This kind of story adapts itself to the child's writing ability. For some children to

write: "I climbed up a mountain" is a major achievement and completely acceptable. Such a story might evoke a response from readers that would encourage the child to expand on this initial statement. Other children might develop extensive and detailed narratives around the same topic. The level of ability and interest of the child determines how far each story is developed.

Teachers have been encouraging the incorporation of details in the story-telling that the child might not give in speech, eg location in time and place, cause, motivation, outcome.

The three-part structure described above also encourages this kind of expansion.

Something happened?
Under what circumstances?
How did it turn out?

With young children these stories are often written over several days and in the

The child begins his story. He selects his colour-coded and visually-cued verb – "climbed". The past tense is used because this is the natural story-telling voice.

The child adds his subject – "I climbed"

The child may add details:

Time and location:

"Yesterday I climbed up the mountain".

The child returns to his story and gives the next stage of his story:

"I fell down the steep cliff and I hurt myself then a helicopter came to rescue me."

Each stage is a complete story

Project teachers would argue that it is easier for a child to write such a narrative than to develop generalised assertions like, "I can read".

light of comments from the teacher and other children in the writing group. This also encourages the incorporation of detail.

No writing programme should deny to any child the opportunity to write on anything he or she wanted. Within the Project many children wrote long or short stories of their choice.

All the writing that a child does should not be seen to be concerned with the teaching of writing. Children should be encouraged to write for their own pleasure and satisfaction.

(b) Another way of supporting beginning writing was by using the "grid". The child wrote a story on paper which has been ruled as a series of boxes. The child wrote one word on each box. When the child revised the first draft, minor revisions could be made within the box such as corrections of spelling, punctuation or vocabulary. If there had been a serious breakdown in meaning and the piece had to be redrafted the child simply cut out the offending section and a new section was stuck in. A child's writing might consist of several chunks of writing stuck on the page. The child could make a final version if the teacher thought this to be necessary.

The grid was not used throughout the Project but a number of teachers were enthusiastic about it and all writing in their classes was done on the grid. It had certain minor benefits, such as the maintaining of spaces between words and keeping writing on a straight line. For some reason it seemed to produce longer pieces of writing but that may reflect the attitude of the teachers.

The important thing about the use of the grid is that it demonstrated again that the written version of the child's story was not sacrosanct. The important things were the composing of the stories and their eventual redrafting if necessary. Teachers were prepared to use various methods that decreased the labour of redrafting and in this way help to encourage the habit.

PHASE FOUR

Each of the phases has its dominating concern.

Phase One had been concerned with encouraging the child's willingness to communicate using a number of techniques.

Phase Two had been concerned with building up story-telling skills and the incorporation of writing characteristics into these. It had also seen the start of letter formation.

Phase Three had been concerned with the child beginning to write.

The work of these phases continues and Phase Four is concerned with **building up of narrative skills in writing and with the extension of the shapes available to the child**. Most importantly was the move from writing being used for story-telling to writing being used in the exploration of themes. The discussion of this is important and will be taken up fully in section 10.

(a) drawing:

The move from talk and drawing to writing brought with it an inevitable contraction in the child's ability to express and communicate experiences and responses to these. This can be a frustrating time and the Project sought to help the child through this by continuing with the drawing programme and with the teacher's scribing of the child's stories.

The developing drawing skills of children enabled them to produce sequences of drawings to support narrative or to produce drawings which concerned themselves less with the individual child and more with the child within a group.

Drawing can be used to help children select things to write about. One technique that we found to be successful in the project was to ask children to draw, on a small scale, a familiar object, cut it out and use it as the basis for a picture-story. For example the drawing of a lollipop, coloured and cut-out was the start for each of the three pictures, (but it could as easily have been a fly, ball, bucket, ladder, firework, puddle, bird, nail, etc.).

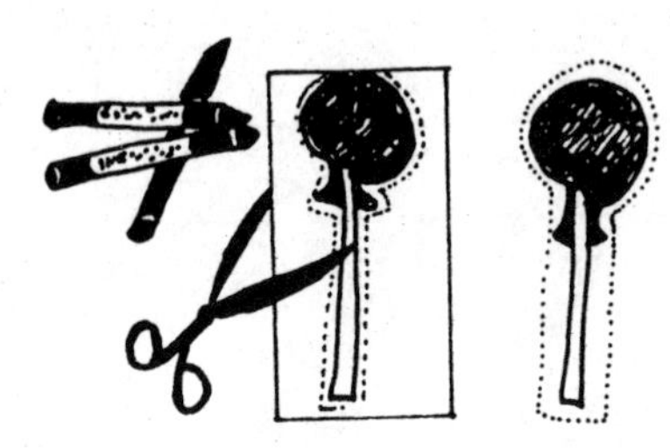

In each case they provided the children with writing opportunities to say what was not apparent in the pictures.

Did the friend like the lollipop? Was she given it or did the children share it? When did it happen?

What happened after the lollipop fell in the dirt? Was it left or was it taken and washed?

Did everyone choose to buy a lollipop or did some of the children prefer other sweets? Which flavours do people like best? How long do they last? Are they good value for money?

As can be seen the emphasis is less on an event and more on the human context.

Another development in drawing was for children to make large size figures of children and adults. These were put together in some situation, say, waiting at a bus stop or outside a shop.

Children decided what these characters might be saying and attached balloons to their mouths with the words in them. This was particularly useful in identifying topics for longer pieces of writing.

(b) plasticine modelling:
Plasticine modelling, the use of characters and backgrounds also continued. It was useful to identify characters who developed definite personalities of their own and could appear in a kind of serial. It might be a brother or sister, a pair of "bad" boys, a bossy man or woman. The teacher could ask the writing group what the characters might be doing on Saturday or what kind of story they would be involved in today. This writing for known characters helped the children find things to write about that little bit easier.

(c) story-books:
Story-books were popular at this stage especially with less able children who were helped to find things to write about and supported in the writing. Even competent children liked them and would fill each page of the book with various events within a continuing story.

(d) picture cards:
Picture cards were used quite extensively at this stage although some teachers did introduce them earlier. They were specially drawn pictures which depicted a scene familiar to children. Many teachers extended the idea by the use of pictures from magazines. Some pictures depicted the single child involved in some incident, trousers caught in barbed wire, facing a large dog, dripping wet, etc, while others showed the child involved with other children, waiting at a bus stop, playing games in the street, meeting strange children, etc.

Three types of writing seemed possible using picture cards:

the child might use the picture to talk about his/her own physical or emotional feelings in a familiar situation;

the child might use the picture as the central event in a three-part narrative;

the child might use the picture to look at events through the eyes of one of the characters in the picture.

The pictures were introduced within the writing group. There was just sufficient discussion to allow children to recall similar events in their own experience and for the teacher to ensure that every child had something to write about. Extensive discussions seemed to increase the problems of the selection of things to write about for the less able child rather than decrease them.

(e) report writing:
As the children were writing more and more within themes teachers began to help children handle report writing.

As has been seen earlier this is a form of narrative. The child has to let people know what s/he was observing or investigating and give his readers some idea as to what had been discovered.

Teachers worked on this within the group taking as the starting point what people might wish to know about what the children had been doing. This took quite a bit of work. The main problem was that children again assumed that their readers knew what they were about and that there was no need to tell them. As the teacher was seen as the reader, and as she set up the activity, it was difficult to get children to think of other, less informed, audiences.

Since children were not telling a story but using a time sequence there was some difficulty in the child's recall of all those stages in the observation or investigation that might have been of interest to readers. The child's lack of experience or stage of intellectual development might mean that the conclusions were not always adequate but it was important that they should be included and that they should be his or her own.

The report became established in most classes alongside the story as part of the child's repertoire of shapes which helped to organise experiences.

(f) writing forms
The involvement of writing in theme work meant that the child might use a number of writing forms. Many of these were based on a time sequence – letters, instructions, were common. Not much time was spent on the formal aspects of these. What was more important was that they served their purpose in a clear and well-ordered way. Here the possibilities for discussion within the writing group was important in deciding what it was that readers would need to know or the effectiveness of pieces produced by children within the group.

Non-narrative writing, eg adverts, notices, impressionistic writing, were to present problems in the selection and organisation of items. Again the problems were presented to the group for discussion and resolution.

PHASE FIVE
This phase continues activities already present. Much of the writing will be within themes but children's personal writing will continue. Such differences in objectives which are identified here depend on the growing maturity of the child and less on linguistic development.

The new objectives which may now be considered are –
(i) writing about experiences from **points of view other than the child's own** or considering the significance of his or her experiences.

(ii) imposing shapes on writing which are **logical rather than chronological**;

(iii) using writing to support **speculation or problem-solving**.

No new material was introduced. The Project however provided suggestions for themes which offered a wider variety of writing purposes.

A number of these were concerned with problem-solving, e.g. "The Park" – turning derelict land into park: "Police!" which involves children solving crimes: fantasy themes of the "quest" type where children encounter various problems.

By Phase Five children are beginning to engage with all the aspects of writing which are relevant to the primary school. Work beyond Phase Five is unlikely to introduce any new elements. For many children the work of Phase Four and Five will continue throughout the primary school. By the end of these five phases the children should be able to write legibly and fluently. They should be able to use writing for a variety of purposes, either for personal expression or to support investigations and themes.

In this writing children should be able to report with some precision on experiences or their responses to them. Some children may be able to look at experiences from points of view other than their own.

Some children will begin to organise their communications logically as well as chronologically.

These skills will have to be developed primarily through the child using writing within certain contexts and with access to helpful feedback from the teacher and other children. Extensive reading will help the child appreciate how writing functions.

All of these skills and awarenesses allow children to find and impose meaning on their experiences. These writing skills do not simply allow children to respond to past events; they enable them to make sense of events with which they are curently involved and to anticipate future events.

Teachers were convinced that children's ability to think their way through things and to find answers to problems had been improved by their mastery of the written language with the precision and variety of organisation which it offers.

10. WRITING WITHIN THEMES

Once children have developed even a limited writing ability this can be employed within thematic contexts with less emphasis being given to the one-off story although this would continue simply because children like writing them. As suggested earlier, other communicative techniques can also be used – drawing, plasticine, etc.

The possiblity of themes of a quite extensive nature and which might involve children over several weeks being sustained by scribing, drawing and other communication techniques had not been developed by the Project directors until certain teachers demonstrated how effective this could be. This meant that themes of a quite demanding nature could be seen as occurring within P1 and providing a purpose for the use of the various non-writing activities described in Phases One and Two.

It would be easy to see the Project as providing a body of material which simply taught in a more effective way, the basics of writing. That is, the ability to form letters on paper. To accept such a view of the Project material is to still give a low status to writing and to the teaching of writing. There was a significant difference in writing ability between children in classes where the teaching of writing was seen as a skill activity unconnected with the wider work of the class and children in other classes whose teachers encouraged them to use writing within contexts which defined a wide variety of writing tasks and purposes. It was one of the strengths of the Project that such comparisons were possible.

The types of themes developed during the Project differed radically from those themes commonly used with young children. Teachers might ask what was to be achieved by children spending a great deal of time exploring the life of a postman, a shopkeeper, a garage mechanic, an ice-cream man? This could be done through "People Who Help Us".

What did children learn from tackling the problems posed by turning derelict and vandalised property into a public park?

The SCOLA Survey(December 1975) listed the themes which were undertaken with older classes in the primary school and the Project directors sought from Project schools information about themes they worked with at the early stages.

It was difficult from the list of themes to find an underlying rationale in the choice of themes and there was little sense of a coherent and developing programme. This is not to say that individual themes might not lead to excellent work and that children might not engage with these themes in an enthusiastic way. It was, however, difficult at times to find the criteria on which the selection and ordering of these themes were based.

Teachers appeared to have favourite themes, ones which had worked or which children had enjoyed. Themes were based on aspects of experience in which children were supposed to be interested. This sometimes led not so much to a child-centred programme but to a programme based on what adults thought children might be interested in. The children's involvement with some of the Project themes showed that they had the capacity to be interested in somewhat unlikely subjects.

The reasons teachers gave for the selection of themes were all perfectly reasonable ones but a clear view of what they saw themes achieving did not emerge clearly. Perhaps that underestimating of the ability of children, which many teachers now declared had existed, contributed to the choice of themes. Perhaps there had been a failure to recognise the adult nature of many of the concepts involved in even child-centred themes with the result that children learned at best only half-truths from their work with them.

This need to provide thematic contexts for writing led the project directors and teachers to consider three things:

(a) the criteria for selection of themes;
(b) the concept of the neutral context;
(c) the integrative role of writing.

(a) Criteria for the selection of themes:
What did we want to do with the young child?
Throughout this report there have been numerous references to meanings. We want the child to live in a meaningful world; a world that makes sense.

If it makes sense, then the child is at ease in the world and feels that it is understandable and ultimately controllable.

How does the child make sense of the world?

Not by being handed pieces of information about the world but by exploring, investigating, responding to, thinking about the world and forming his or her own model of the world.

This is a model which will keep altering as the child has to accomodate new data or insights.

The school will make available to children significant experiences and give them access to significant data.

It will help children develop awareness and skills which enable them to engage with the new experiences and problems with which the world will continually present them.

In looking for possible situations and contexts the Project team took as their base a number of awarenesses which they would wish to develop in the young child.

(i) awareness of the self:
This is in all the Project material with which the child is involved from the time he/she enters school. All the early material of the Project permits children to record their experiences and their responses to them. One of the main lines of development in the writing tasks set children is their increasing ability to be aware of themselves in the various situations in which they find themselves.

(ii) awareness of the child in time:
One of the earliest Project themes helps the children reconstruct their lives as babies; record and evaluate, as far as possible themselves now; anticipate their future as big boys and girls – the ability to swim the length of the baths, ride a bike, tie their laces, go to the shops themselves.

As Tony the Ice-Cream man drives his van he sees the changing seasons and how nature and people relate to them – as well as being an ice-cream man!

In "Old Smith's Place" the children's contemplation of a vandalised old house leads them to contemplate the nature of the life once lived there.

(iii) awareness of the child in space:
Again much of the early Project work has to do with the child's awareness of his/her own environment which is recorded and explored through various media.

For example, the theme "The Street" looks at the child's involvement with his/her immediate environment and the opportunities and problems it presents. There is material on school, waste land, parks.

(iv) awareness of other living creatures:
Much of the material looks at the child within a family. Themes such as "Jim the Postman" and "Tony the Ice-cream Man" involve him/her in contructing and exploring the lives of people s/he knows and who in their turn touch on the on the lives of many other people. "Sam the Cat"; "The Day Mother was Ill in Bed"; "The Baby" ask the child to adopt a caring position – the position of having to be responsible for other living beings, some of whom are small as s/he is small. In building "The Park" the child has to consider the need of all kinds of people who might wish to use it. S/he has to consider that someone is responsible for everything s/he sees around them.

The themes touch on the roles of many people but in a natural way. They are looked at when they touch the child's life – shopkeepers, police, doctors, vets, councillors, park keepers, teachers, tradesmen. The child's growing ability to look at experiences through the eyes of others is stimulated by a series of picture cards in which the child is asked to consider various incidents in which the behaviour of children may effect others.

(v) awareness of the physical laws that govern the universe:
Starting in the pains and pleasures of bathtime "Water" develops into an investigation of the properties, uses, even the aesthetics of water. Starting in the child's running on it, rolling on it, digging it and playing with it "Earth" looks at its properties, the way it is used or abused and the creatures that live in it.

(vi) awareness that we live our lives according to certain beliefs:
Running through all the themes is a strong awareness of our need to have concern for those living creatures who share our world and for that world itself. In festival themes, like "Christmas", there was an attempt to persuade the child that there is more to the festival than presents, parties and food.

These awarenesses are returned to constantly as the children deepen their experience and their ability to make sense of a complex and changing world.

(b) The neutral context:
The role the Project saw for itself was different from that of the teacher who set children to copy from the board. The Project saw itself creating opportunities for the children to write and showing them how to write. It did not see itself as telling the children what to write.

The various environments presented to the child in Phase One or Two are like stage sets. It is up to the child to provide the actors and the action.

The picture cards are moments of frozen action, stills from a moving film for which the child writes the script. They are not the old sequence of child kicking ball/broken window/ child running away/angry man – Write the story.

They are two groups of children contemplating each other, a child searching for something in long grass, a baby crawling on the floor, a group at the bus stop.

It is the child who cries "Action!" and causes the still figures to start moving.

The Project themes were not about factual information or the opportunity for expressive activity. They start with the knowledge and capacities that children bring through engaging with a manageable portion of the environment and these are used to extend their understanding at their own level. This takes place through questioning, observing, investigating and recording. The development of the theme is not exclusively in the control of the teacher but also develops through the ways in which the child responds. The teacher's role is to question and pose problems rather than give answers.

It is hoped that the awarenesses listed above will be developed and that the child will aquire certain skills, particularly those of language and problem-solving.

The Project themes are of certain kinds.

One is the children's **building up of the life of an animal or person** as in *Sam the Cat* or *Jim the Postman*. This is the *Mr Togs* type theme.

There is the **investigative theme** – water, earth, light, sound, air.

There is the **problem-solving theme** – what will we do with this derelict land in the middle of the housing scheme – it's a public disgrace!

how will we rescue the sad princess?

how will we cross the dangerous land?

how will Tony turn this van into an ice-cream van?

There is the **observation theme** – this links with the investigative theme but is more concerned with aspects of nature as in *Tony and his Ice-cream Van* which has a strong element of observation and recording in it.

There is the **anthology** or **magazine theme** – these can be useful short themes as *"The Day Mother was Ill in Bed"*. Write her a get-well card; write down your favourite story for her or make one up; write the instructions for a game she can play in bed; the recipe for a meal you can prepare; instructions on how to carry out household chores; an amusing incident if Dad takes over the housework; a conversation between you and the doctor's receptionist as you give details of you mother's illness.

We have our awarenesses and we have a repertoire of different kinds of themes.

What about starting points?

These are close to the child. A child lies down on the floor while others draw round him or her. The outline is pinned to the wall. The teacher pins a baby's garment in the middle of it. This is the start of the *Child in Time*.

Who likes bath-time? Who doesn't?

This is the start of the *water theme*.

The teacher pins up a newspaper. Inserted in one of the advertising columns is an advert offering a kitten to a good home.

Would we like a kitten? How do we reply? How will we collect it? Who knows how to look after cats? What will they eat? What do they need?

This is the start of *Sam the Cat*.

There is a frieze of a house in a derelict estate; it's a mess. Round the edge begin to appear faces with bubbles coming from the mouths shouting protests. Hands appear grasping placards. Protests have turned to action.

This is the start of turning *"Old Smith's Place"* into *"The Park"*.

Children need things that their imaginations can work on.

There has to be a cat – a toy, a cardboard cut-out, an old fur.

Jim the Postman has to be life-sized. Then he can make his daily rounds to letter boxes set up in the school and have a post-office to return to.

Tony has to have a van made from old boxes. It should have "working" bits. Things should open, turn, lift.

The children spending money on the park had a catalogue and "real" money which was banked with the teacher. They could draw from this £5 and £10 notes which had to be exchanged for equipment.

Will we hand over £400 for a lavatory or a new fence?

Where relevant, children worked with friezes. As *"The Park"* was built up so the frieze was altered.

Sam had a frieze showing a simple house interior with the things a cat would like and a frieze showing a bit of the garden.

Jim had a frieze of a street which he visited. The shops and houses were populated by the children.

While the children made many of the suggestions themselves the teacher could make things happen.

When the children came in Sam's frieze might show some feathers and some blood!

The park Children might receive letters from BMX riders protesting they had nowhere to go now the Park had been prettied up.

Mrs Grant's milk bottles hadn't been taken in. What will Jim do? What will he find?

These themes were easier to manage in some ways in that they didn't demand that the teacher collected a great deal of factual material beforehand. **She had to have the ability to pose problems or ask questions and let the children get on with solutions and answers**. If special knowledge was required the teacher would help them to get access to it. The teacher might demonstrate techniques for making the frieze, building the van, expressing something effectively in writing. The material of the theme was no longer completely within the knowledge of the teacher. It was a vehicle for the child's own experiences, imaginings and speculations.

(c) Writing and integration:
The Project was interested in themes because they provided contexts which defined purposes for writing, gave opportunities for different types of writing, and provided content for the writing.

The Project might start by saying, "Well, it would be good if the children could write a report about what they've done or if they could write a poem on their response or write instructions for someone to follow."

Attention was on writing.
What had not been considered deeply enough was that behind these forms of writing were various personal skills that were called on when the child wrote.

The child writing an impressionistic piece of prose was drawing on sensitivity to colours, movements, shapes, sound, etc.

A child writing from the point of view of someone else was drawing on social awareness and the capacity for sympathy.

The child writing a report was drawing in his/her capacity for the identification of significant detail and his/her ability to put things into an acceptable sequence.

The child writing down his solution to a problem was drawing on his/her capacity for thinking and for projecting that thought into a situation which s/he hadn't even experienced.

When teachers asked a child to write within a theme s/he was projecting into that theme not just writing skills but all the personal skills, awareness and capacities that the child had.

That was what bowled over the Project directors when they walked into certain classrooms.

That is what excited teachers and made them say that a new dimension had been added to their work.

When children wrote about "*Water*" they went well beyond the normal environmental studies investigation.

They engaged with the theme of water through memory, imagination, observation, response, perception, thought.

Integration is more than involving the various subjects of the curriculum in an investigation. It is involving the various aspects of a child's personality in that investigation with various forms of writing providing the channels through which this was done.

Of course in certain themes like "*The Park*" a certain line of development had to be followed but that was usually quite simple to evolve. This was the trunk of the tree; writing still provided the branches and the fruit.

Examples of writing

Children in P2 were investigating the physical properties of various items in their environment. Here they are examining water.

The pieces of writing are some examples of different uses of writing within the investigation; they do not represent all that was done.

Report on an experiment:

On Friday afternoon we put water in ice-cube containers and put it in the freezer in the kitchen. On Monday the water had turned to ice. We did an experiment with the ice-cubes. We put two on Sally's hand, two outside and two on the widowsill and waited to see which one melted first. The two on Sally's hand melted first and then the ones outside. The ice-cubes on the windowsill took the longest time to melt. The ones on Sally's hand melted first because her hand was warm. The ones outside melted second because it was a warm sunny day. The ones on the windowsill melted the slowest because the window and plants were stopping the sun from getting at the ice-cubes. Sally's hand was red and cold because the ice-cubes were freezing. I think the plates that the other ice-cubes were on were cold too.

Story seen from another person's point of view:

Splash! The old lady's foot landed right in the puddle of water. It was bucketing down with rain. She had just been to her friend's but it started to rain as soon as she stepped out. It started light but then it got harder and harder. The old lady felt unhappy because she was wearing sandals and summer clothes. She had been to the shops before she went to her friend's as she had a lot of shopping. The shopping was heavy. She didn't like the rain because it hurt her hands very much. Her back was hurting because the shopping is too heavy for her to carry.

Descriptions of objects known to children:

A sponge is soft and round. It has holes and bubbles to squeeze water out. You need soap on it to clean yourself. It is made of foam.

A shower has got a hose and a tap so that water can come through. You stand under it and lines of water spray on to your head.

Story on imagined incident: interesting use of "flashback"

Paul felt miserable and unhappy. He was cold too, very cold and wet. Paul looked like he had a bath. His clothes were wet and cold. Paul's shoes were soaking wet. Everytime he walked round, bubbles came out of his shoes. His socks were white before, but now they were greyish. All of his legs were covered in goose pimples. He could hardly walk home to have a warm bath.

Paul had been round the pond. He did not see two big boys following him. When he looked around he saw the boys coming closer and closer. They came up to him. They took a hold of him. They counted up to three. They went "one, two, three" and there was Paul in the pond with a big splash. The two big boys were calling Paul names. Paul was not happy at all. The big boys were running away from Paul. Then Paul saw a stick in the water. He swam to it and managed to swim to the side. When he got home, his mum said, "Where are you going?" Paul said, "I am going upstairs to have a bath." Mum said, "All right, but quickly." Paul had a bath. Then he came downstairs. His mum called her husband. He gave Paul a smack on the bottom and sent him to bed with no supper. Paul was crying.

Varying reports on properties of liquids:
The Liquid Race
In class today we ran a race between syrup, oil, shampoo and water. We put some of each on a tray when we tilted the tray and the water came running down. The cooking oil was second, and shampoo was third and last of all was the syrup. The water was first because it is smooth then and very runny. The syrup was last because it was very thick and sticky and cannot go as fast as the water.

Sad Mr Syrup
We ran a race between Mr Water, Mr Cooking Oil, Mr Shampoo and Mr Syrup. Mr Water came first, but poor Mr Syrup came last. That is why Mr Syrup was sad. He was always last in the race. We all tried to cheer him up. We said that he could be better at something else. Besides he was better looking because he was gold coloured. He tasted better because he was so sweet. We told him that we put him in cake more often than water. Then he was happy. Mrs M....... said he should write about him, but nobody wanted to. But now we have and he is happy. The End.

Mr Syrup can do this	*Mr Water can do this*
cooking	*keeps us alive*
baking	*wash us*
smells nice	*water the flowers*
tastes nice	*wash the car*

Attributes list:

Bottles are small	*Bottles are blue*
Bottles are fat	*Bottles are glass*
Bottles are thin	*Bottles can smash*
Bottles are green	

Instructions:
Instructions for baby's bathtime:

1. *Make sure the baby's bath water is not too hot or cold.*

2. *Don't fill the bath too full.*

3. *Make sure you have everything ready towel, talc, soap, cream, shampoo.*

4. *Take off baby's clothes.*

5. *Make sure when you put the baby in the bath you don't let go of her.*

6. *Wash baby with baby soap.*

7. *Wash baby's hair making sure no shampoo gets in baby's eyes or mouth.*

8. *Lift out the baby and put her carefully on a towel.*

9. *Dry baby and put her carefully on a towel.*

10. *Put on baby's nappy and clothes.*

11. *Put baby to bed*

Precautions:
You must be careful or you will burn yourself.

You must always hold the kettle with the handle.

You must make sure that there is water inside the kettle.

You must not touch it by the sides.

You must have dry hands before you put in the plug.

You must not play beside the kettle.

Poetry:
Snow
Snowflakes fluttering
Snowflakes dancing
Snowflakes floating
A white sheet.

Freezing hands
Red feet
Children playing
Children sliding
People grumbling
People mumbling
I like the snow.

White sparkling snow
Soft in my hand
Roll it and pat it.
Make a snowball.

Cold hands
red hands
crinkly hands
Hold a snowball.

Wet slushy snow
Cold mushy snow
My snowball has gone.

Rainstorms
Black clouds above
Rain bouncing off car roofs
Windows shattering
Thunder vibrating everywhere
Lightning striking trees
Lightning flashing
Chimneys falling off roofs
Rain pouring down
Plumbers trying to fix everything
People shouting
Babies crying
Puddles flowing down drains
Plumbers drills pounding
Photographers camera clicking
Not scared of thunder
Well, just a wee bit.
Counting seconds between one flash then another.
I like rainstorms.

Speculation:
If a house were flooded it would be horrible. The carpets would be squelchy and soft. The wall-paper would be peeling off the wall. The windows would be smashed and the door would be swelling up. I wouldn't like to live in it ever again. I would try to tidy it up. The carpet would be dirty and sticks and stones would be lying on the new carpet we've got. The skirting board would be all cracked and falling apart. The electric things wouldn't work including gas things and the phones. It would be terrible having a house like that. The pipes that join onto the toilet would be blocked.

Opinion:
Why I don't like bathtime
I don't like bathtime because when I go in the water is hot but then soon gets cold. I don't like feeling cold and shivering. I like the shower better because it is much quicker. You can wash your face and hair better in the shower. I think. I don't like the bath because I am too big for it. I like the bubbles but not the bath. In the shower I can play with a helecopter and pretend it is raining. In the bath people play with toys and I don't like it because it is babyish and I'm grown up now.

Sense impressions:
Water – cold and tasty for a soldier on the march.

Oil in a can – gooey and smelly to mend the car.

A flask of chicken noodle soup – hot and beautiful at a picnic.

A carton of milk – white and creamy for my breakfast.

Tea in a pot – yellowy brown and dripping to drink with a biscuit.

Coke – good and fizzy when I'm in bed with a sore head.

Hot water bottle – cozy lying in bed at nights.

A bottle of bubble bath – lots of bubbles and smelling of strawberries for my bath.

A spray perfume – lovely like spring flowers smell to go to a party.

A glass of beer – brown and bubbly for my Dad in the pub.

11. SIGNIFICANT CHANGES IN TEACHERS' PRACTICE

As teachers and Project directors met to discuss the joint experience of the Project, teachers identified those new awarenesses about writing which they felt had led to significant changes in the way in which they approached the teaching of writing.

(a) A new status for writing:
It was generally agreed that writing now had a importance within the curriculum that it had not previously enjoyed.

One important reason for this was the teacher's understanding of the relationship between the written language and the child's thought processes and the improvement in child performance that had come from this.

Bringing the child's writing within contexts instead of it existing as an isolated skill-acquisition had led to the child's closer engagement with the material of the themes being investigated and had given the work of the class "a new dimension".

As outlined in the discussion of Phase Four the written language had acted as a unexpected integrative force and had led to a variety of curricular activities being involved quite naturally in thematic work.

The realisation that many activities, especially independent, expressive activities, could contribute to the child's mastering of writing had led to such activities being given a new importance and approached with a greater degree of seriousness.

The involvement of children with a meaningful and purposeful approach to learning to write had led to significant changes in the child's attitude to writing. Teachers declared that for the first time they had classes that wanted to write and individual teachers remarked in the fact that children were choosing writing as an independent activity. These were reports of children being sent away from the classroom to work within a writing group and the teacher's new expectation that this activity would be treated seriously and that children would return to the classroom having produced an acceptable piece of writing.

(b) Definition of the teachers' role:
Many teachers who had talked with the Project directors at the beginning of the Project had spoken of their uncertainty about their role in the teaching of writing. This uncertainty had gradually disappeared as teachers worked within the Project material and began to acquire new understanding about the nature of writing and its acquisition.

Teachers were more able to define their writing objectives at any particular stage in the first three years of primary education.

Many teachers who had talked with the Project directors at the beginning of the Project had spoken of their uncertainty about their role in the teaching of writing. This uncertainty had gradually disappeared as teachers worked within the Project material and began to acquire new understanding about the nature of writing and its acquisition.

Teachers were more able to define their writing objectives at any particular stage in the first three years of primary education.

Teachers had a clearer understanding of the nature of the response they should make to the child engaged in writing.

Teachers had some sense of development phases in the child's learning to write and could both respond to the writing child and anticipate his/her likely future difficulties.

Teachers began to see their role in the child's learning to write being redefined. It was not enough to stimulate writing and then evaluate the product; the child had to learn about the processes of writing. The teacher had to make available to the child her expectations about how one set about writing and to share with the child that mastery of writing techniques that she had acquired. Teachers could now see their role as that of the "master writer" working with "apprentice writers".

The teacher and child had to be more prepared to work with how the child constructed his story and not solely with the storyline itself. The comments made by children in P2 writing groups demonstrated that they were capable of picking up criteria for the criticism of the writing of other children.

(c) Writing is a group activity:
This was one of the most radical changes that teachers had to make but it was essential if the child had to get that support s/he received as a member of a conversation group. There was too much for the young child to acquire on his/her own and the teacher had not the time to become involved in a continuing one-to-one relationship within the group.

Again, the analogy of the child learning to speak is a useful one.

Who taught the child to speak?
The other speakers with whom s/he came in contact.

Similarly, the teacher had to enlist other writers in teaching the child to write.

Who were these writers?

(i) There was the child her/himself. Each time a child reached for his/her rubber, or scored out or started again, s/he was measuring his/her performance against certain expectations of what writing should be like. By sharing her expectations the teacher widened and deepened these expectations. It would seem desirable to develop the child's capacity for self-criticism. There would seem to be some value in not having the teacher the sole source of evaluation. Other children can say what they consider to be successful, interesting, amusing, etc in a child's writing and also those things they didn't like.

The child him/herself can be asked to identify what s/he considers the good things and the bad things in his/her writing, the parts that didn't quite come off. The next time s/he he writes s/he can be asked to pay particular attention to those aspects of writing s/he has identified as creating difficulty.

All writers have to practise their craft, not in workbook exercises but in the refining and enhancing of the text itself.

(ii) Then there are the other children in the group who provide an audience, act as a support, criticise, evaluate, share ideas and skills.

A writing group is not simply an organisational convenience, a group of children sitting together, it is a group who come together for a common and serious purpose and to pool those skills and awarenesses that they have.

Eventually the child must turn from the group and confront the blank page but even in P7 there is no reason why this should not be done within a group with whom the child may share the delight of something well-said and to whom s/he can turn for advice when the writing falters and stops.

(iii) The teacher, as we have said, is the *master-writer* who will share her knowledge with the children who are still apprentice writers.

There is an attractive word for that body of knowledge which is the province of the craftsman as well as the man of religion – "the mysteries".

The teacher initiates the child into the mysteries of writing.

Many children have little idea of what people do when they write. One effective way of showing this is for the teacher to sit down with a writing group and write on a topic similar to those tackled by the children. The teacher talks her way through the writing, saying why she chose to start where she did; why she preferred one word to another; what she was trying to achieve there; how ideas are held together.

There are few activities outside teaching in which the instructors would not be prepared to demonstrate to learners their own mastery of the craft yet teachers too often try to teach through letting children copy or through rules and prescriptions which are often not helpful to children because children have had little part in formulating those rules.

(iv) There are dozens of skilled writers in every classroom.

There are the authors of books to which children should have access. These authors are master craftsmen. In reading, the child communes with the adult writer. There may be stories or characters which grip him/her and which s/he will wish to recreate in his own terms. The child may begin to appreciate how one sets about being an author, how experience can be shaped and organised in writing. Some children seem to subsist on a diet of reading scheme books and course books. They will learn little from such a poor diet.

The classroom should be saturated with reading material. There are simple books for chidren to read for themselves; books to look at; cassettes to listen to; adult helpers or older children who can read to the children. The young writer is entering a great fraternity/sorority of writers. The child him/herself, the teacher, adult writers, other children can all show him what one does to become a writer.

(d) Seeing writing from a child's point of view:

A child-centred approach to writing is often seen a selecting topics for writing which are relevant for children.

Teachers working within the Project became aware that many of the writing tasks set depended upon an adult perspective, and created considerable unanticipated difficulties for the children.

(i) It is not common for a child in conversation to be expected to recall a past experience without a great deal of support from his listeners. On the other hand, it is assumed that children will be able to tell stories and, in fact, in conversation the child's story may be his longest unbroken piece of language. Much of the writing set young children is the recall of experience. As has been stated several times, the Project concentrated on *story telling*.

(ii) A common example of this is the newstime type of story.

This poses all kinds of problems for children.

There is the problem of recalling past events.

There is the problem of selection – what is it that people will want to read about?

There is the problem of organising all this in an accessible form.

(iii) Within the Project when children were asked to compose a story they were asked to select the action first of all. Finite verbs, in the past tense, like "climbed" have a strong narrative impetus and it is quite easy for a child to build up a story round about these which reflect his/her own experience. Much of the writing produced by young children seems to be influenced by the teacher's desire to simplify the demands made on the children by limiting vocabulary choice or minimising spelling problems. This can lead to stories of the following kind:

I can swim.
I like chips.
I am four.
I have a new bike.

These are easy to write but they are not stories. They are generalised statements or assertions. It is easy for an adult to develop these but it is more difficult for the child.

Project teachers reported an increased understanding of those capabilities that children brought to the writing task and of the difficulties which these tasks contained for them.

(e) Change in emphasis:
In teaching writing there had been concern with letter formation, sound/symbol relationship, phonic values and so on.

The creative writing movement had drawn attention to the expressive elements in writing. Previously teachers might have paid attention to vocabulary elements. Project teachers now paid increased attention to the significance of the way in which the child organised meaning in the sentence and of the overall shape imposed on his/her writing.

Teachers were more sensitive to what was going inside a child's writing and a child will only develop as a writer if s/he is also aware of this.

(f) Anticipating the child's development as a writer:
The years of working with a greater volume of children's writing made teachers more aware of the nature of writing – the differences between talking and writing, the various components that made up writing skill, the separation into composing and secretarial skills.

One important outcome of this was that teachers accepted that some skills and awarenesses relevant to writing could be taught in non-writing activities. This helped define more precisely the way in which teachers related to such activities.

It also helped teachers anticipating possible areas of difficulty.

The change from responding to writing to anticipating writing was a significant one.

Through these new awarenesses teachers were better able to answer the following questions:

What am I trying to achieve at this stage in the child's learning to write?

What knowledge or skills does the child bring to this that I can build on?

Have I any right to assume that the task will be meaningful to the children, relevant to their experience or within their intellectual capacity?

What are the difficulties in the writing task likely to be and can I anticipate them?

What kind of situation or context will stimulate the child to write and provide a purpose for writing?

What kind of response may I make that will be helpful to the child?

When teacher looked at a piece of children's writing she could say with greater clarity "Where do we go from here?"

12. QUESTIONS TEACHERS ASK

When teachers who had not worked with the Project material met with teachers who had, certain questions were asked:

(a) Why was it necessary to change your way of teaching writing
Project teachers said they had been uncertain about their role in the teaching of writing and they welcomed a new approach. Having worked in the Project they were convinced that not only did children's writing improve but so did children's performance in other curricular areas.

(b) How do you find the time?
The realisation that one to one teaching in the teaching of writing was not always necessary and also the alternative activities that the Project developed occupied children for longer times and much more purposefully. The Project also made us aware that a number of other classroom activities contributed to the teaching of writing. The Project team always stressed that writing was not a separate activity that had to be superimposed on existing activities.

(c) Did you have to give up anything?
Project teachers agreed they gave up certain things whose principal purpose was to keep children busy but no important element of the curriculum had to be neglected.

(d) Didn't the Project take away resources from other things?
The Project approach is comparatively inexpensive. There is an increased demand for writing paper of better quality as that facilitates the development of handwriting skills and for various forms of writing instruments which produce a fine line.

Schools could obviously benefit from the provision of listening centres but cassette recorders could be used.

The Project material exists partly as an exemplar and partly as a classroom resource. It would be possible for teachers to adapt the ideas contained within the Project material to meet the particular needs of their own classes but in some cases this would be time-consuming and would not produce such durable material.

The package is important in getting teachers launched into this way of working. It gives them plenty to do and compensates for those things they may have to give up.

One of the most articulate and enthusiastic supporters of the Project who had started off quite unconvinced about its validity gives as her advice "Take the material, follow the instructions and work through it for a year. Children will come to no harm through this. At the end of the year you will appreciate what the Project's aims are and if they are acceptable to you. You will then find you can work within your own material, adapting it to the aims of the Project."

(e) Isn't it difficult to change to teaching writing as a group activity?
Project teachers said that provided the teacher and class were accustomed to working in groups this wasn't so. There was a gradual introduction with children coming together for drawing or handwriting and these groups later became writing groups. The Project made suggestions as to how children would be selected for groups, outlined the teacher's role in groups and suggested various group activities. The movement to group writing was never sudden and was always supported by the Project material.

13. IMPLEMENTING THE REPORT IN SCHOOLS

The Foundations of Writing Project report sets out to give teachers an understanding of the nature of writing, how writing skills are acquired and the relationship between writing and learning. It is hoped that this will enable teachers to teach writing effectively to young children.

For many teachers this may mean significant changes in their practice. Individual teachers may see value in some of the suggestions made within the report and may seek to incorporate specific items in their teaching.

It is only when all teachers in school have an agreed understanding about the nature of writing and a knowledge of how to teach it that there will be real development in children's writing ability.

(a) Introducing the report to a school

All members of a school staff, including nursery, should be seen as being involved in creating a "writing policy" for the school.

All members of staff should know about the report but the implementing of the report should not be left to individual teachers.

It is the responsibility of the headteacher to place writing on the "agenda" and to indicate how school-based in-service will focus on writing throughout the school.

(b) Review of present practice

The first stage in implementing the report will be the review of current practice within the school. The work of the Project showed the necessity for a frank questioning of assumptions about writing and its teaching.

In departmental and staff meetings teachers might discuss such questions as:

What opportunities do you give children for writing?

Do chidren in your class produce a variety of writing?

How do you organise writing at present?

How do you normally repond to children's writing? (The group's discussion of actual samples of writing is always beneficial.)

What is the attitude of children in your class to writing – is writing enjoyed or is it greeted with a groan?

What is your estimate of the writing ability of children in your class?

(c) Using the report

It is probably better for teachers meeting together to discuss sections of the report rather than to consider the whole.

Headteachers or Assistant Headteachers might designate aspects of the report to be discussed.

The following points might form the basis for discussion at in-service meetings:

handwriting;
the difference between speech and writing;
group teaching of writing;
teaching writing in curricular contexts;
learning writing through using writing;
the teacher's role in the teaching of writing.

(d) The identification of significant changes

After their discussion of their own practice and the examination of the report the staff of a school might identify what changes must take place and then move to examining how the school might cope with those changes.

Matters like disposition of staff, utilisation of space, organisation of classes, curricular changes, relevant material, might be discussed.

It is important that once implementing begins within the classroom that teachers are encouraged in this implementing and that they should feel that their work is valued and supported by other members of staff.

The work of the Project demonstrated that a determining factor in the success or otherwise of using Project approaches was the involvement of promoted staff in the introduction of these approaches. The role of the assistant headteacher was seen as critical as mediating between the project and the class teachers.

It is also vital that teachers are encouraged to accord a new status to writing, to see it as a central activity in the curriculum which has a beneficial effect on most curricular areas.

(e) The material

When teachers have discussed the report they should then see the material as being supportive of what they wish to do in the classroom. Although the material will provide plenty of things to do and will help a teacher make that move to the strategies suggested by the report, the project is not essentially about material. It is about understanding how children develop as competent writers and teachers should extend or modify the material to fit in with themes or investigations being undertaken in her classroom.

The material was used least effectively when –

teachers picked bits and pieces of material which fitted in with previous practice and did not introduce a coherent and developing writing programme;

when teachers superimposed the Project on the normal work and did not incorporate Project approaches in the ongoing work of the class;

when teachers simply worked through Phase One and Phase Two material as if it were a collection of isolated activities and did not see the various expressive activities as a series of techniques through which children could engage with the recording and communicating of their experiences.

Departmental meetings might examine and discuss the use of the material and how it relates to the various developmental phases outlined in the report.

Obviously the handwriting programme will have implications for the teaching of handwriting throughout the school.

(f) Talking with parents

Project schools held meetings with parents to explain the project to them. Parents may expect that school will teach writing in a certain way and it is important that they should be informed about changes about to take place. Children may bring home a different form of work or may report on things they are doing which are unfamiliar to parents.

These meetings were well-attended and the Project was well received. The opportunity was taken to talk about the teaching of reading and writing and how parents might support the work of the school. It is important that the school is very specific about the nature of the changes they intend to introduce. The distribution of a statement outlining the sequence of activities and how the child might move on from one to the other was helpful. The teaching of handwriting was one area where the practice of the school might differ considerably from the way in which parents taught their children. Project schools were prepared to let interested parents borrow handwriting cards so that there was co-operation between school and home.

Parents seemed to respond well to being taken into the confidence of the school and in most cases useful co-operation was established.

Most schools meet with parents of new intakes prior to the children coming to school. This might be the time to begin to talk to them about writing and to ask for their support.

If parents are not invited into school on a regular basis there would be some advantage in the Assistant Headteacher bringing parents into school, perhaps on at least two occasions in the first year, to look at the progress being made. This might be in small groups.

(g) School-based in-service

It is obvious that the report cannot be implemented without there being a programme of school-based in-service. Schools will tackle this in-service in different ways but from it should emerge an agreed whole school policy on writing and clear guidelines for the implementing of that policy.

Curriculum innovation can be limited to its effect if a teacher has to work on her own, picking up ideas from a report, and perhaps with the feeling that some colleagues are not in sympathy with what she is doing.

Teachers need support from within the school and from the Advisory Service and the Education Authority if meaningful development is to take place.

The Project was fortunate to receive that support.

Innovation is more successful if it develops from within rather than is imposed from without.

Innovating teachers have to feel that they can influence and shape the new developments and that what they do is satisfying to them and valued by their colleagues.

Foundations of Writing embraced the principle that the school is the focus of its own development. Its style of curriculum innovation sought to make effective bridges between the artificial issue of whether in-service should be school-based or centrally led. The ideas promoted by the Project, some familiar, some new and challenging to teachers, were introduced by leaders from outwith the school sector. But the Project ensured that teachers were involved throughout, not as functionaries, but as partners who could initiate ideas and suggest methodology, give of their own valuable expertise as well as learn from the Project Directors. For any innovation to be effective teachers must first be convinced that change is desirable and that in the course of the innovation they are able to influence its development.

Influenced by the ideas of the Project, teachers and Headteachers made decisions about changing their children's experience of writing. They altered classroom organisation, reviewed the status of writing within the curriculum; re-allocated teaching time and became critical of their previous expectations. How this happened varied from school to school as each teacher made tentative and then more confident matches between her current ideas and practice in writing and those predicated by the project. Some of the ways in which the pilot work encouraged this positive commitment to change might therefore be significant for its wider dissemination.

Teachers in the Project were encouraged to think for themselves and to ask questions

They were helped to be more conscious of their existing stances on writing – the status they gave it/the materials they used/ the experiences they provided. Decisions about changing their practice were then based on the belief that the project ideas offered something better. The quality of this comparison of existing and new practice varied from school to school. In each case, however, it significantly influenced the change and sustained teachers through the difficulties of re-organisation and methodology which they encountered as they worked towards making the project ideas their own. Wider dissemination of the Project approach should take account of the importance of teacher/ school commitment, as outlined above, as the major factor in curriculum change.

Teachers in the Project were valued as researchers, problem-solvers and evaluators

The Project did not set out to be "teacher proof". The Project team outlined core principles about writing, and about children's experience in writing. They also provided materials through which an approach consistent with this view of writing could be developed. Teachers were then encouraged to use their skills of judgement, of analysis and of reflection. Wider dissemination of the project should recognise the need to encourage and support such skills.

FOUNDATIONS OF WRITING PROJECT

STEERING COMMITTEE (1981–1986)

† May Barclay (Convener)
Head Teacher (from 1984)
Burdiehouse Primary School
Edinburgh

†*William Jackson – Project Director
formerly Principal Lecturer in English, Hamilton College of Education

William Michael – Project Director
Principal Lecturer in Art, Jordanhill College of Education

* Joyce Eddie
Assistant Head Teacher (to 1984)
Cults Primary School
Aberdeen

Vera Hearl
Assistant Head Teacher (from 1984)
(Early Education)
Muirfield Primary School
Arbroath

Maureen Lamont
Adviser in Primary Education (from 1984)
Grampian Regional Council
Moray Division

* Elaine Melvin
Head Teacher (to 1984)
Annette Street Primary School
Glasgow

Sheena McArthur
Adviser in Early Education (from 1984)
Tayside Regional Council

Heather McLeod (from 1984)
Teacher
Seafield Primary School
Elgin

†*Claire Milne
Adviser in Primary Education
Tayside Regional Council

Frank Adams
Principal Curriculum Officer (Primary Education)
Scottish Curriculum Development Service

Ray Dely (Secretary)
Curriculum Officer (Primary Education)
Scottish Curriculum Development Service

* members of Scottish Committee on Language Arts
† member of Development Group on Language Arts

FOUNDATIONS OF WRITING PROJECT

SCHOOLS INVOLVED IN DEVELOPMENT WORK

GRAMPIAN REGION
Moray Division

Elgin East End School
ELGIN

Hythehill Primary School
LOSSIEMOUTH

Mosstodloch Primary School
FOCHABERS

Pilmuir Primary School
FORRES

Seafield Primary School
ELGIN

PRIMARY ADVISER – Maureen Lamont

The Project is grateful for the personal contribution made by Mr R. Duncan, Assistant Director of Education, Grampian Regional Council

STRATHCLYDE REGION
Lanark Division

Biggar Primary School
BIGGAR

Calder Street Primary School
MOTHERWELL

Leadhills Primary School
BIGGAR

David Livingstone Memorial Primary School
BLANTYRE

PRIMARY ADVISER – Joan Munro

The Project is grateful to Margaret Jackson, Department of Primary Education, Jordanhill College of Education, for her work in Project schools in Lanark Division.

TAYSIDE REGION
Angus Division

Hayshead Primary School
ARBROATH

Muirfield Primary School
ARBROATH

Warddykes Primary School
ARBROATH

PRIMARY ADVISER – Claire Milne

TAYSIDE REGION
Perth & Kinross Division

Breadalbane Academy Primary School
ABERFELDY

Crieff Primary School
CRIEFF

Goodlyburn Primary School
PERTH

Tulloch Primary School
PERTH

PRIMARY ADVISER – Sheena McArthur

FOUNDATIONS OF WRITING PROJECT

SCHOOLS INVOLVED IN EVALUATION

The Project is grateful to the following schools which took part in a small scale evaluation of material produced by Project schools elsewhere in Scotland.

Bankier Primary School
Banknock
Central Region

Banton Primary School
Kilsyth
Dumbarton Division
Strathclyde Region

Fairlie Primary School
Fairlie
Ayr Division
Strathclyde Region

Fencedyke Primary School
Irvine
Ayr Division
Strathclyde Region

Kilmaurs Primary School
Kilmaurs
Ayr Division
Strathclyde Region

Lainshaw Primary School
Stewarton
Kilmarnock
Ayr Division
Strathclyde Region

Moorpark Primary School
Kilbirnie
Ayr Division
Strathclyde Region

St Mary's Primary School
Cumbernauld
Dumbarton Division
Strathclyde Region

Silverknowes Primary School
Edinburgh
Lothian Region

Tinto Primary School
Glasgow
Strathclyde Region